TAKE CHARGE OF YOUR

VIEW

Vision Insight Engagement Will

658.3124
P

NeXus Impress Publishers, Newton, MA

For information about special discounts for bulk purchases, please contact NeXus Impress Publishers Special Sales at info@nexusimpress.com.

Cover design by Jasmina Misic

X, 172 : ILL

Edited by Sari Boren and Deborah Sosin

1 2 3 4 5 6 7 8 9 10

Library of Congress Cataloging in Publication Data Library of Congress Control Number: 2017906879

ISBN (print) 978-0-9861342-0-3 9000

"What is the work for us to do in our short time here?"[1]
—Bruce Springsteen, in his best-selling book, Born to Run

For Jack, Kayla and Jared—
who bring joy and companionship to the journey

Table of Contents

CONTENTS

Map of Your Six-Week Journey

WEEK 1	WEEK 2	WEEK 3
VISION	*INSIGHT*	*ENGAGEMENT*

VISION for your life and how your work fits in

Outcomes
▸ Reflections on past and present
▸ A Vision Statement

Daily Practice
▸ 60-second intention in the service of your **VIEW**

Gain self-awareness and **INSIGHT** that will help you achieve your vision.

Outcomes
▸ Best Self and Signature Skills
▸ Feedback and feedforward from 3 trusted people
▸ Brief action plan

Daily Practice
▸ 60-second reflection on lesser strengths

Boost **ENGAGEMENT** in your job through activities in the NEXUS.

▸ Feel more flow

Outcomes
▸ One work aspiration
▸ Your Company's VIEW
▸ Your NeXtivity

Daily Practice
▸ 60-second "scan"

WEEK 4	WEEK 5	WEEK 6

WILL

Strengthen the **WILL** to bring vision, insight, engagement to life.

Outcomes
▸ Remove one barrier to your **VIEW**
▸ Your Mentoring Network
▸ One 60-second mind-body practice

Daily Practice
▸ 60-second "quality"

RECRUIT

How to Recruit your Manager to support your **VIEW**

Outcomes
▸ Your Pitch
▸ Empathy Map
▸ Recruit you manger

Daily Practice
▸ Build a better relationship with your boss

Your VIEW for Life

TAKE CHARGE OF YOUR

Career Advice You Won't Get from Your Boss

INTRODUCTION
VISION. INSIGHT. ENGAGEMENT. WILL. [VIEW]

These are the new skills for taking charge of your life and career in the 21st century. Do you know how to make them work for you?

This is your personal guide to creating your VIEW. On an average weekday, you will spend more time working than any other single activity, more than sleeping, caring for others, eating or relaxing.[2] So you need to ask yourself: What brings meaning and purpose to your life? How does work fit in? If you are currently working, are you spending your hours the way you want? Can you deploy your passions and talents in your work today, live the life you want to live? Does your work prepare you for the future?

Together, we will take a six-week journey and I will help you answer these questions. As a leadership coach and culture change consultant who's worked with hundreds of people in coaching sessions and workshops over seventeen years, I've heard many people express their dreams and frustrations when it comes to their career paths. Maybe one or two of these reflect how you feel:

"I know what I want in my life and career but don't know how to make it happen."
"I feel stuck."
"I've lost the passion for my work."
"I'm burning out."
"I work so much there's no room for anything else—like a life."
"I'm really unhappy and don't know what to do."
"The politics here get in the way of creating the work I really want."
"I can't talk with my manager about my vision for my career and the work I care about."

On these pages, I'll share the secrets for mastering the process of how to take charge of your self-directed career. When you self-direct your career, you follow your VIEW to create the work opportunities that are meaningful to you but also advantageous for your employer, customers and clients. You seek and create situations that are win-win.

Should I take this journey?

You should take this journey if you want to learn how to deploy your passions in your work situation today, to create the life you want and the work you love. If you are self-employed or between jobs, I'll offer tips for how to tailor the tools to your situation. This is not a job-hunter's manual. Through the six weeks and 18 experiences, you'll gain the mind-set, tools and relationships you need to master the four skills throughout your lifetime:

- **VISION** is your personal picture for what you want from life and how work fits in—a gut feeling about what's important to you. You feel so strongly connected to this picture that you're willing to work toward making it happen.

- **INSIGHT** is self-awareness of who you are at your best and worst, and your impact on others. This includes your values, personal qualities and Signature Skills, both as you understand them and as others experience them in you. With true INSIGHT, you bring more of your Best Self to the world and know what you want to change or improve upon in yourself in service of living your VISION.

- **ENGAGEMENT** is your skill in creating work opportunities that are both meaningful to you and aligned with the purpose and goals of something you are part of, whether you work for an organization or for yourself. You take charge of creating this sweet spot—what I call the NeXus—where your VIEW intersects with the VIEW of an organization, customer or client. The greater the overlap in the NeXus, the more fully engaged, energized and absorbed you feel, a state of mind known as flow.

- **WILL** is your capacity to choose your mind-set, feelings and actions with intention. It isn't enough to dream and reflect on your VISION and INSIGHT, or to take a few steps toward ENGAGEMENT. The strength of your inner resources of WILL, including mind-body connection, makes them happen. This doesn't mean you're alone. On the contrary. When you lean on your Mentoring Network, you find strength from the circles of people you bring together for mutual exchange of ideas, feedback, practical resources, new connections and support. You help one another build WILL.

In Weeks 1–4 of this journey, we'll focus on one of the skills of your VIEW. In Week 5, you'll get tips for how to talk to people who can help you create your VIEW, including your boss if you work in an organization. And, if you're not sure you can get what you need from your current situation, we'll go through a checklist of questions to help you think through whether to stay or move on to greener pastures. But first, we'll focus on making the most of where you are now, to bring the best of yourself to your work today.

This is your personal journey for living the life and doing the work you were born to do.

YOUR VIEW: THE NEW SKILLS FOR CAREER AND LIFE IN THE 21ST CENTURY

The stories you'll read throughout the six weeks are based on the the true experiences of leaders and managers I've worked with throughout my career. But I've changed names, industries, genders and even mixed some of their stories together so you could learn from other people's experiences without compromising the confidentiality of those who gave me their trust.

On any journey, each person starts from a different place. Here are stories people have told me in both one-on-one coaching sessions and workshops. You'll hear more about some of these stories throughout the book.

Mary, *a division director in a global telecommunications company, struggled with how to create a clearer VISION for her life and work. The CEO asked her to take on broader levels of responsibility in the latest company restructuring, but her gut said it wasn't the right move at this midpoint in her career. Her predicament was part of a broader pattern. "When I look back over my career, all I see is a patchwork of jobs," she confessed. She frowned and described her ambivalence. "To be honest, I didn't feel passionate about any of them."*

Sanjay, *a manager in a biotechnology company, lacked INSIGHT, the self-awareness everyone needs for success. His VISION was to take on increasing responsibility and have a seat at the table with key decision makers. Sanjay thought of himself as a big-picture thinker, but other people said he worked too much in the weeds. "I'm very strategic," he said. He couldn't figure out what was holding him back. When I asked his colleagues for feedback and for their perceptions of his performance and how he could improve, they said he was detail-oriented but that he overused that strength.*

Robert, *a high-level administrator at a leading healthcare organization, needed a path to ENGAGEMENT. He loved working in healthcare, which satisfied his VISION for a meaningful career related to healing. He'd gained INSIGHT about his skills that were strengths, but the people who provided feedback on his strengths and areas for development noticed that he seemed to have hit a ceiling in his career. "I don't know where to go from here," Robert confided. To create a breakout opportunity where he could shine as a leader, Robert needed to pitch win-win activities that would boost his visibility and skills while making an impact on both the organization and the people it served.*

Michelle, *newly promoted president of a nonprofit, had worked with me for five months. She'd created a VISION for her life and career; she had gained INSIGHT about strengths, areas for improvement and impact on others. She had even created a practical plan for greater ENGAGEMENT in her role, which included specific activities where she could shore up her leadership skills and create a win-win for herself and the organization. She knew what she wanted and needed to do, but each time we met, she reported feeling stuck. When I asked, "What's the barrier?" she gave a knowing smile and confessed the fears that were holding her back. She struggled with the WILL to chart the path forward.*

Career self-direction is the ongoing process of visualizing the life you want and creating a work path that aligns with your VIEW. This research-and-practice-based concept is the foundation of your self-directed career. Whether I am coaching an executive in the C-Suite or facilitating a leadership and career workshop for managers and employees, I meet people who want to be their best selves. They want to learn new skills, prepare for the future and find meaning in their work. My father was my first role model for taking charge of my VIEW.

My father worked for one company, Uniroyal, Inc., for his entire career. He was born in an industrial Massachusetts city, Worcester, on the third floor of a three-family home that locals like to call a "triple-decker." The house was perched on a hill crowded with immigrant families from southern Italy. When he was nine, he made holiday ornaments from birch trees and candles and sold them to customers on his paper route to help his family pay for groceries. When it was time to go to college, the Massachusetts Institute of Technology (MIT) accepted him into the freshman class. But his family couldn't afford the tuition or dormitory fees, so he had to turn down their offer. Instead, he lived at home and attended a local college, Worcester Polytechnic Institute, or WPI, where he studied chemistry. The stress of working and going to college full time overwhelmed him. He dropped out, served in the United States Marine for three years, then returned to WPI. At the beginning of his junior year, an amazing thing happened. Uniroyal gave him a full-tuition scholarship. At graduation, he looked up at his father in the stands, waved his diploma and shouted, "I did it, Dad!"

Eleven companies offered him a job, but he chose Uniroyal's offer. "They had been so good to me," he told me later. He and my mother said goodbye to their families and the triple-deckers and relocated to Uniroyal's factories in the town of Naugatuck, Connecticut. (If you've ever had the pleasure of sitting on fake-leather fabric called Naugahyde, now you know where it was made and how it got its name.)

My father rose quickly from chemist to plant superintendent. I was 14 years old when Uniroyal moved our family overseas to Rome, Italy, where he led the organization's Italian operations. My brothers, Paul and Joe, and I went to classes at an American overseas school. After three years, we returned to Naugatuck just as Uniroyal shut the doors on the rubber factories.

Looking back now, I realize that my father's career was caught in a big change in the relationship between American companies and employees. In Naugatuck, people believed that a job with Uniroyal was a job for life. But career choices narrowed; job ladders shrank. The company issued pink slips, termination notices. My father was one of the lucky ones. He didn't get a pink slip, but he also didn't get promoted. For his career to advance, he would have had to leave and go to another company. While that's very common today, it was almost unthinkable at the time. He stayed at Uniroyal out of loyalty, but he had to learn how to stay relevant and create his own work opportunities. It was brand-new territory and there were no role models or roadmaps to guide him. He'd once dreamed of being in the C-suite, the offices of the CEO and other people, with the title of "chief," but he found career and life satisfaction by creating his own opportunities. As it turns out, my own career path, helping leaders and their people bring their best selves to build great companies, is part of my DNA.

How is your father's story relevant to taking charge of my career today?

> **TIP >YOUR VIEW:**
> **A TIMELESS RESOURCE**
>
> Like you, your VIEW changes with each passing year. I hope this guide becomes a personal resource and cheerleader that you return to again and again to touch base, refresh where you are, or to help as you move to a new organization, job or life phase. Wherever you are in your life or career, we'll take this journey together.

WELCOME TO CAREERS 3.0

The pace of change today is coming at us at a rate that is 300 times faster than the transition to the industrial age, say experts at the consulting firm McKinsey,[3] faster than any other shift in human history. Like my father, we have few role models and roadmaps. We call that Careers 3.0.

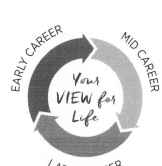

Today, careers progress along a cycle. You could begin a new career at the age of 22 or 62. Your VIEW is crucial to guiding your choices and opportunities, whatever your age or career stage.

In Careers 1.0, from about the early industrial era to the 1980s, people stayed with one employer and the company determined their career moves, which were like climbing a job ladder. In Careers 2.0, from the mid-1980s to 2000, people like my father stayed with their employer but created their opportunities from different job ladders. Some people described it like a career lattice or jungle gym.In Careers 3.0, today, the thinking changed to "we are all self-employed," as career guru Cliff Hakim predicted in the 1994.[4] Jobs will be short lived as companies emerge, grow and decline in shorter time spans. This means that we are all entrepreneurs, staying relevant and creating work opportunities whether we work inside an organization as a regular employee or externally as a consultant or contractor.

What do these changes mean to me?

- At times throughout your life and career, you may choose to work either as an external consultant or as a regular employee. You may find your perfect job in an organization or create it on your own.

- If you choose to work for someone else, you want to work for employers who support your professional development. You want to do work that is meaningful to you now but that also prepares you for the future. This is especially true if you are a Millennial, born between 1994 and 2000, because you may hold more than 20 different jobs in your lifetime, including those you create.

- You have more peer-to-peer support and learning networks available at your fingertips than ever before. Social media platforms encourage information sharing and professional support. You want to know how to access and take advantage of these resources.

- Your age is no longer equal to a chronological stage in your career. With people all over the world living longer, futurists like Mary O'Hara-Devereaux predict you'll have two middle-lives! This means you could begin a brand-new career at the age of 22 or 62.[5]

Taking charge of your VIEW is a personal experience. I'll guide you through a roadmap for your six-week journey comprised of 18 total experiences, approximately three per week, to help you get started.

Why six weeks?

That's just enough time to get the big picture, experience how each part of the VIEW builds on the next and begin to implement actions. It takes at least 30 days to acquire a new habit and our goal is to build lifelong skills. A practice is "a behavior done again and again with the intention to improve," says James Flaherty, the founder of New Ventures West, co-founder of Integral Leadership LLC, and the author of Coaching: Evoking Excellence I Others.[6] Even if you don't have the time or energy to take the deepest dive, you'll get nuggets of learning and a daily practice to help you acquire lifelong habits for creating your best life and work.

Speaking of time, what's the pace? How much time should I commit?

Go with the program: If you'd like to see what you can accomplish in six weeks, go at the recommended pace. Focus on one capability per week. Follow the suggested timing for each experience. You can always take a deeper dive and come back to something later.

Go slower: If you'd like to take time to absorb and digest, complete one capability every two weeks instead of every week to make the journey deeper.

Go faster: If you'd like to speed through and just get the gist, skim the entire program in one week. Think about your answers instead of writing them down. Tab the pages where you might want to take a deeper dive, and come back to them at a later date.

Go with your gut: If you prefer your own path and don't like being confined by someone else's model, ignore the above and go at whatever pace or approach works for you.

It's all good, whatever you choose. On the next page, you'll get the full overview of the six weeks, so you know what to expect.

Do I have to go through the six weeks in order?

I highly recommend going in order since the ideas build from one week to the next and you'll get the most of the whole experience. But maybe you are looking for a quick hit of relief and just want to find a little guidance to help with a specific challenge you are facing. If that's the case, this list of shortcuts may guide you to the tips and ideas you seek now:

If this sounds like you and you feel an urgent need to address the situation:	Then go to:
"I feel lost and don't know what I want in my life and career." *"I work so much, there's no room for anything else—like a life."*	Week 1: VISION
"The politics here get in the way of creating the work I really want."	Week 2: INSIGHT
"I've lost the passion for my work." *"I'm burning out."*	Week 3: ENGAGEMENT
"I know what I want in my life and career but don't know how to make it happen." AND/OR *"I'm really unhappy and don't know what to do."* AND/OR *"I feel stuck."*	Week 4: WILL
"I can't talk with my manager about my vision for my career and the work I care about."	Week 5: FIRST, RECRUIT YOUR BOSS

I recommend completing each week in sequence. But this is your VIEW and your journey. You are the one in charge.

YOUR CREATIVITY

You learn by reflecting on your experience, not by doing, as legendary educator John Dewey once said. The 18 Experiences are designed to help you learn from your real-world experience.

Each week you will:

 Think... *Through reflections, you will learn from experience.*

 Feel... *Use your emotions as a practical, useful part of your mindful self so you get clear about what you need or are experiencing*

 Do... *Commit to one practice, so you see real change and progress*

YOUR FIVE COMMITMENTS

Before we launch our six weeks together, make a vow to yourself to get the most you can from this experience. Pledge allegiance to yourself by making these five commitments:

Your Commitment *I WILL...*	Encouragement
1. *set up the physical space and environment that will allow me to read, do the activities and think freely beyond the day-to-day.*	What is the best time and place for your self-reflection? Starbucks? A quiet corner in your home? The beach? The bus or metro? You don't have to travel to Italy, India or Indonesia like Elizabeth Gilbert, author of *Eat, Pray, Love*, to create your best environment. Although, I'll admit, it worked pretty well for her.
2. *find an accountability partner, such as a friend, spouse or colleague who will check in, challenge and help. Maybe this person wants to learn with you and experience the six weeks together.*	This book is your guide to career fitness. Like taking an exercise class, it can help to have a workout partner. You act as a sounding board for each other, connect each other to people or resources or simply listen when you each want to think out loud. Here's an analogy: A lot of people choose to exercise with other people. Why? When we exercise with other people, we are less alone, more engaged and push ourselves and our partners to perform our best.

3.	*invest at least 45 minutes each week and schedule the time in my daily or weekly calendar, even if it is only in 10- to 20-minute blocks.*	"Hope is not a plan," as the old saying goes. If you don't make the time, you won't find the time in the crush of your daily commitments and activities. You may have to sacrifice something to make room. For example, if you watch an hour of television a week, you may wish to reprioritize that activity.
4.	*make an "If-Then" commitment.[7]*	Even when you have done everything possible to set up the right time, environment and support, things don't always go as planned. That's where an "If-Then" commitment can help. For example, imagine IF the 30 minutes you scheduled at 6 a.m. for this work gets consumed by another commitment—the kids wake up early, the dog gets sick, you have to travel for business. THEN you could look at your schedule and find 15 minutes at some other point in the day. It's not the full commitment, but it keeps the ball rolling! Thanks to the folks at the Center for Creative Leadership for this idea.
5.	*be open to new experiences.*	Research shows that people who are open to new learning experiences are happier and more fulfilled than people who believe they have nothing to learn. "Open" people believe that qualities are *things you can cultivate through your own efforts; success is about being your best self, not about being better than others,"* says Carol Dweck, author of the groundbreaking book *Mindset*. Through research, she found that happy, fulfilled people who live their own definition of success have a growth mindset. Fulfillment and growth elude people with a fixed mindset, who believe that "qualities are carved in stone." Choose a growth mindset and you are fulfilling your VIEW.

> *Now you are ready to begin*

TIP >MAKE IT MUTUAL!

Find a partner, such as a friend, family member or colleague and go through the journey together. You could check in, listen, challenge, be accountable to and support one another.

PART 1

Vision & Insight

Dream & Reflect

Vision

is your personal picture for what you want from life and

how work fits in, a gut feeling about what's important to

you. You feel so strongly connected to this picture that

you're willing to work toward making it happen.

Vision

FEATURED EXPERIENCES:

1 Your Story, Your Path

2 Your Future

3 Your VISION

VISION Wrap-Up, Reflection and Practice

WHEN YOU WERE YOUNGER, what did you want to be when you grew up? Perhaps you dreamed of being a rock star, a dancer, a teacher, a police officer or a professional hockey player. When my brother Paul was five years old, our neighbor, Frank, helped him grow his first garden. That crop of tomatoes ignited his passion for farming. Just as he completed a PhD in plant sciences at the University of Minnesota, a friend introduced him to organic farming and Paul hasn't looked back since. Today, he is the respected farmer of a popular organic farm in western Connecticut. But, at the time he first pursued his dreams, organic farming was on the fringe of the agricultural industry. Paul was a pioneer in his field because he had the self-awareness to know he'd never be happy in an agricultural lab. As farmer, he not only produces amazing, locally grown vegetables, he champions sustainable agriculture. In a recent documentary filmed on Paul's farm, the camera closes in on Paul's contented smile as he explains how he has felt about his career: "Every night when I walk these fields, I feel grateful to be living my vision."

"The view you adopt for yourself profoundly affects the way you lead your life." —Carol Dweck, author of *Mindset*

Erin Judge is a red-headed comedienne with a "plus-sized figure." "I'm beginning to understand that I'm beautiful 500 years ago, so I replaced my bathroom scale with a large clam shell," she said during our interview, laughing. She was referring to the Italian Renaissance painting, The Birth of Venus by Sandro Botticelli. Erin's complex childhood influenced her career. "We moved from Brooklyn, New York, to Plano, Texas, when I was nine years old and I didn't fit in," she said. Isolated, Erin turned to television for comfort, watching Comedy Central and trying to make friends at school by repeating jokes. Years later, when she applied to PhD programs in American Studies, she realized her admissions essays were all about her interest in comedy. She launched her career on campus, doing stand-up routines and meeting famous entertainers who encouraged her to pursue her unique brand. "As a kid, I would repeat other people's jokes. When I started writing and telling my own jokes, I discovered my career." Today, a comedienne and writer who performs all over the world, her comedy has a social mission to tear down stereotypes and encourage acceptance. Erin loves her work and it shows on her face. "My first wrinkle is a laugh line," she told me.[8]

Paul and Erin have a lot in common. Each has a self-authored VISION that compelled them to make unconventional choices without role models or roadmaps. Who they are is what they do, and their professional lives are fulfilling. You'll notice, though, that they are both self-employed. If you work in an organization, you might be wondering what's relevant about their stories since, most likely, other people set goals for you and you must be accountable to those people. The answer: everything.

For one thing, you may long to connect your job to a greater purpose or you may wonder how to reclaim some of the joy of your early dreams. In my travels, I've worked with many kinds of professionals who could trace their career choices back to an early age.

For example:

- Scientists who knew from their first microscope kit that they wanted to cure cancer.

- Hedge fund managers who ran lemonade stands at the age of seven.

- Academic deans and professors who realized they loved learning as soon as they could read.

- Physicians who grew up feeling their purpose was to heal and bring hope.

This week, like every week, you will do Experiences that encourage you to think, do and feel. If you'd like a refresher on this approach, revisit the Five Commitments in the Introduction. Here are this week's Experiences:

Think·Feel·Do

 Interview yourself about your VISION. *In Experience #1: Your Story, Your Path, you reflect on a brief series of questions that will encourage you to reflect on your past as well as the present. The questions will encourage you to* **think**.

 Create a visual picture of your future. *In Experience #2: Your Future, your answers to the first Experience will help inform what you want from your life both today and tomorrow. The picture will encourage you to* **feel**.

 Draft a Vision Statement. *This is the culminating moment of the week. In Experience #3, you will draw upon your thoughts and feelings from the "think and feel" experiences and summarize them into a brief paragraph of your VISION for your life and how work fits in.*

Why

- This is your chance to think unconventionally and dream as big as you wish.

- Writing focuses your thoughts and forces you to be more specific and concrete about your ideas.

- A clear picture of what you want in life is both a touchstone for choices you will make and an inspiration for moving forward.

Outcomes for this week:

- Reflection on where you are today and where you have been.

- A picture of your VISION for your life and how work fits in.

- A written statement of thoughts and feelings that you can revise and refer to throughout the six weeks.

VISION EXPERIENCE #1: YOUR STORY, YOUR PATH
Time: 30–60 mins.

> ❧ **WHAT TO DO: Your life is a story in which you are the main character. What path brought you here? Interview yourself. Read the questions on the following pages and write your answers when you see the cue, "Your Turn."**

Intense focus, incubation and distraction are all part of the creative process, so it's OK to work for 15–20 minutes and then take a break.[9] For best results, write your answers. Writing is a tool. It makes your thoughts specific and concrete and leaves a record you can build upon from week to week.

Find time and a quiet space. Think big. There are no right or wrong answers and no one is listening. Let go of judgment and let your answers flow. There are three parts to this personal interview: 1) Begin with the past; 2) Reflect on the present; and 3) Imagine the work of your dreams.

Let's get started.

1. Begin with the past.

Joy

> ❯ *What gave you joy in your youth? Is it still in your life? If not, do you wish you could reclaim it?*

Reflection: Experiences of your childhood that brought you joy—drawing, music, participating in science club, doing sports, being outdoors—may be clues to your inner sense of self and purpose. Adulthood and the practicalities of everyday life may have forced you to leave these behind.

Your Turn: *This is what gave me joy. It is/not in my life today:*

_____

_____

_____

Dreams

> *What did you want to be when you grew up?*

Reflection: What was your answer when grown-ups asked you that question? What appealed to you about that job or vocation? Your dreams may have influenced choices you've made. You may have forgotten about these dreams, but maybe they haven't forgotten you. Perhaps there's a calling you feel you missed out on and it influences your work satisfaction today.

Your Turn: *This is what I wanted to be. It is/not in my life today:*

_____

_____

_____

Family

> *What did your parents or guardians do for work? How did they influence your career choices?*

Researchers from Boston University conducted a groundbreaking study, among the first global studies of career development trends across countries. Over time, they tracked the career satisfaction and progress of 200 people and found that families have a profound influence on our careers because our early family life shapes our values.[10] What was important to your parents may influence your work values and choices today. Do you value achievement over satisfaction? Self-fulfillment over financial security?

Reflection: My father's career and our family's experience influenced my work passion and choices, as I shared in the Introduction. How did your family and their experiences influence yours?

Your Turn: *My family influenced my work passion and choice . . .*

_____

_____

_____

Life

2. Reflect on the Present:

> *What matters most in your life? What is the one most important thing?*

_____

_____

_____

Reflection: Some coaching clients struggle to answer this question for a surprising reason: The answer came quickly and they worried about the meaning! Here's a great example:

"What's the one most important thing in your life?" I asked Brianna, a nonprofit executive who was looking to make a change.	*"The gym," she said. "I'm a little embarrassed about that answer. It seems shallow."*
"Well, why is the gym your one, most important thing?" I asked.	*"To keep myself healthy," she replied.*
"And why is that important?" I asked again.	*"To keep my mind clear and my body functioning well."*
"And why is that important?"	*"So that I can bring my best self to my family, friends, work and community."*
"And why is that important?"	*"Because this is the vision for my life: bringing joy and support to others."*

All that from a gym! Now it's your turn.

Your Turn: *Here is what matters most in my life: It is the one, most important thing . . .*

_____

_____

_____

Now ask yourself:

Why?

_____

Why?

_____

Why?

_____

Keep asking yourself, "Why?" until you strike oil, an answer that resonates from wells deep within. If you don't like your answer today, then come back tomorrow or next month. Life is fluid and changing, and there is value in learning from change.

Heros

›   *What or whom do you admire? What does this tell you about what you want in your life?*

_____

_____

_____

›   *Who is on your personal, top-ten most-admired list? The researchers from Boston University also found that as we gain experiences, friends and colleagues, it causes us to rethink or question the choices we've made.[11] We are also influenced by people we read about, historical figures or people featured in high-profile magazines.*

Reflection: Whose face comes to mind? The people we admire reflect those things that we want for ourselves and our lives. What does this person do? How does s/he live his/her life? What is in this person's life? How does s/he find joy? What does it say about you that you admire this person?

Your Turn: *The person/people that I admire are . . .*

_____

_____

_____

I admire him/her because . . .

_____

_____

_____

Money

> *How does financial wealth factor into your VISION for your life's success?*

Reflection: *"Money is something we choose to trade our life's energy for."* [12]

You get to know a lot about strangers when you're thrown together for four hours in a car.

One day, after leading a workshop for a group of leaders on Wall Street, I taxied to LaGuardia airport, eager to catch my flight back to my family. High winds hounded the streets of New York City and my flight was cancelled. As I milled around the airport entrance trying to figure out what to do next, I met two bankers who were also trying to get back to Boston. We decided to share a car.

Victor and Alan had vice-president titles, wore designer suits, owned suburban homes in Greater Boston and vacation homes on the Atlantic coast. Their wives and children lived in Massachusetts, but they lived in New York City during the work week. As we traveled north on I-95, driving through the congested cities and leafy suburbs, Victor talked about interesting clients, invigorating deals and the marketplace. In spite of working long hours, he looked refreshed and confident. Alan, in an identical job, had dark rings under his eyes and barely smiled for the entire ride. Instead of talking about work, he talked about the hardship of the commute because he only got to spend time with his four children three days a week. Some weeks, he said, it was even less. It struck me that he seemed sad and stuck. Victor talked as if his work fulfilled his VIEW. For Alan, I suspected, the money was costing him his satisfaction in life.

For most of us, work is not a choice: We must give our energy in exchange for a paycheck that enables us to live. What trade-offs are you willing to make? Are you trading off too much today? If you were laid off from your job, would you see it as an opportunity? Do you have a plan for financing your later years or retirement? Think about your answers to these questions as you write your answer below.

‣ Your Turn: *What role does financial wealth play in your VISION?*

_____

_____

_____

These reflection questions have been leading up to a key question that will provide perspective as you take charge of your VIEW and create the career of your dreams.

Work

‣ *How does work fit into your VISION for your life? What work do you need to be doing, regardless of where you are working, to find meaning and to feed your personal dreams?*

Reflection: James was a rising star in an investment banking firm. He specialized in complex mathematics and colleagues sought his expert guidance. When James helped launch the London office, his manager asked him to take on more management responsibility. He felt torn. His professional passion lay in solving seemingly intractable issues. Becoming a manager meant he would have to spend more time managing people and less time being the expert. Also, he and his wife wanted to start a family. Although it was unusual for someone to turn down a chance for promotion, James asked to not be considered. His work choices needed to support the all-important parts of his vision.

Priya, a senior administrative director in higher education, had grown up in a rural town in India where she'd lived with her mother, father, grandparents, aunts, uncles and cousins. Against the odds, she'd put herself through school and worked her way up. When we met, her annual salary exceeded her parents' combined lifetime earnings. She and her husband both worked outside of the home, supporting their two children and their extended family as well. But her job consumed so much of her energy, she felt like she was missing her son's early years. I asked Priya to create a vision for her life and identify how work fit in. This simple activity reminded her of the passion she had for both her family and for meaningful work, and enabled the insight that she needed to delegate more—a win-win for her and the team members who wanted more opportunities to develop.

Reflection: How important is work in the bigger picture of your life? What does work mean to you?

Your Turn: *Here's how work fits into the bigger picture of my life . . .*

_____

_____

_____

_____

Let's pause
for a moment
to ask . . .

How

are

you...

feeling?

You may be feeling all sorts of emotions right now:

- Perplexed about where all this heading?

- A little overwhelmed?

- Worried that your VISION is too grand? Or unclear?

- Concerned that things aren't adding up?

- Excited?

Don't worry, whatever you are feeling is totally natural for where you are.

The first time I experienced a VISION exercise was when I personally sought the help of a career coach. My life felt out of sync. I had just supported my husband through a PhD program at the Massachusetts Institute of Technology (MIT) and we had two little children. I had an interesting job but it was taking over my life. I worried that if I didn't make a change I would never be able to do the work that was truly meaningful to me. Worse, I worried that my children would grow up without having a strong connection with me. Whenever I tried to have a career conversation with my manager, she brushed me aside and said she expected me to figure things out. Not knowing where to turn, I asked a colleague for the name of a career coach. She put me in touch with Ilene Rudman, who works in Greater Boston.

Ilene asked me to close my eyes and then guided me through a VISION experience. I envisioned being the founder of a consulting practice, which was not as common as it is today. In one part of the experience, Ilene asked me to drum up an image of my "Wise Woman," picturing who I am at my best. I had just completed a bicycle race up Mt. Washington, the steepest bike climb in the continental United States. So, naturally, in my mind's-eye, my wise woman wore my purple biking top.

"She's handing you something," said Ilene. "What is it?"

"An energy bar for the soul," I replied, picturing the gold foil wrapping.

"What are the ingredients?"

"Spirituality, courage, love."

OK, it's a little flaky, but the image gave me something to hold on to. The clarity of my vision guided me in creating two more job opportunities in the company, both of which brought me closer to my future. As of this writing, it's been 16 years since I founded Prior Consulting; and I've finished this book, which has taken eight years to write. Today, I am living the results of that first VISION exercise.

VISION. A picture of your life and how works fits in. A picture that you feel deeply connected to and that you are willing to invest your time and energy to make real, however long it takes.

Back to our regularly scheduled Experiences.

VISION EXPERIENCE #2: YOUR FUTURE
Time: 30 mins.

In Experience #1, you reflected on the past and the present. In this Experience, you will envision your future. This may require the opposite of what you are asked to do in your day job, where even the most creative among us is encouraged to think analytically, to get to the point quickly, and to focus on what is practical. I am asking you to cast the practical aside for a few minutes and give yourself the rare chance to dream big.

This next experience may take you out of your comfort zone —and that's exactly the point. On the next page, you will draw a picture or make a collage that taps in to your VISION. Maybe your artistic abilities—like mine—stalled at the stage of stick figures, broccoli trees and starchy rays of sunshine. It doesn't matter. No one is judging your art. This is about your creative expression. There is no right or wrong. It's just you and your VIEW.

In Careers 3.0, living your VIEW demands your creativity. "The MFA is the new MBA," said Daniel Pink, well-known author of Drive and a popular TED-Talks speaker.[13] (An MFA is a Master of Fine Arts degree. An MBA is a Master of Business Administration degree.) Pink says that we live in a digital world where super computers do routine processing that people used to do. "In our competitive and evolving economy, being logical and analytical is no longer enough. Left brain is out. Right-brain noodling, the kind of processing that is intuitive and creative and synthetic, will soon rule the day," the Washington Post reported.[14] At least for now, humans can do something that computers can't: have empathy and create.

James, the investment banker who was offered greater management responsibility, set aside 15 minutes between our meetings to draw two pictures: an image of his life/work "Today" and one of "The Future." At first, he felt uncomfortable with the experience and wondered why the heck we were "wasting time." Later, he told me he got "kind of into it." He chose to focus "Today" on his work life and the image he downloaded will really catch your eye. It features two people, back-to-back, unable to communicate but with an inner desire to have a connection. The picture said a thousand words: James felt isolated from his colleagues. It was a turning point in our coaching because, up until then, he had wanted to talk about the conflict he felt over the offered promotion. We turned our attention away from the promotion and brainstormed approaches that would bring James more satisfying relationships with his colleagues—a win-win for James and the organization. The breakthrough insight: relationships, not achievement, were at the heart of his VIEW.

For his VISION of "The Future," James drew a house with a white picket fence, a dog, cat and family and told me he would always prioritize family over work, as much as his work gave him fulfillment. With those values in mind, we designed a proposal to his manager for how James could move toward his VISION while benefitting the company at the same time. The manager saw the proposal as a win-win and it was implemented.

You'll find James's masterpiece on the next page.

Years ago, Oprah Winfrey, the acclaimed TV host, held a contest in which she asked participants to write down their biggest dream and enter a drawing. One woman asked for all of her debt to be paid off, while another asked for a trip to Disneyworld. Through the drawing, both of their entries won. You would think they would have both been ecstatic, except that the woman who won the Disney trip frowned while she was up on stage, while the woman whose debt had been erased jumped and smiled. As it turned out, the Disney requester also had a lot of debt and would have wished to have it paid off. But she had aimed low and only asked for a vacation. Oprah told this story when she was keynote speaker at a women's conference many years ago. It's stuck with me all these years. We can be guilty of aiming too low, getting what we want, only to realize we wanted something more or different. So, dream big. There are no right or wrong answers to the questions or exercises in this journal—only your ideas and the possibilities.

This is your chance to focus on what you really want. You will land where you aim, so why not aim high?

It's time to begin.

⚜ **What to do:** In this Experience, you will draw two pictures. Your "Today" picture will represent your life today and how work fits into it. Your "Future" picture will represent the life and work you want.

Example:

James's picture of "Today."   *Love, by Ukrainian sculptor Alexander Milov,*
presented at Burning Man 2015

James's picture of "The Future."

ॐ **WHAT TO DO:** Draw a picture or create a collage of your life "Today" in the space below. Like James, you can choose whatever focus you like.

🐾 WHAT TO DO: Draw a picture or create a collage of your life in "The Future." Choose whatever is important to you.

✎ WHAT TO DO: Compare the two pictures and write about the differences and gaps. Write your answers to these questions.

› *What is in your life/work today that feeds your VISION?*

_____

_____

_____

_____

_____

_____

_____

_____

_____

_____

_____

_____

_____

› *What's missing? What do you want more of in your life/work?*

_____

_____

_____

_____

_____

_____

_____

_____

_____

_____

_____

_____

_____

VISION EXPERIENCE #3: YOUR VISION STATEMENT
Time: 30 mins.

Make a commitment by transforming your VISION into a statement.
Here are few sample Vision Statements

"For now, I want to be the best operations leader in this industry while getting ready to start a new career in five years, when I will play a major role in town government."
—George, Operations Leader, Digital Media Industry

"When I am living my vision, I am building myself, my family, my community and my nation. This happens whenever I have had the opportunity to touch someone's life, to help them grow, to build competence, capability, to 'teach them to fish.'"
—Sam, Telecommunications Company Founder

"I've helped create a great company that is built to last. Our people have opportunities to grow and succeed; our shareholders get return on their bets for their faith in us. But mostly, our drugs heal patients."
—Lakshmi, Human Resources Executive, Pharmaceutical Company

"I've started a community center in my father's name: It's a magnet for the youth in our neighborhood and it's making a difference in the life of the community."
—Stephanie, Nonprofit Leader

"My work is fulfilling and I'm making a difference in people's lives through the programs I design for clients and the employees I help. But family will always matter most. I want to structure my work life to support that part of my vision and prioritize relationships over achievement."
—Jane, Consultant, Global Business Services Consulting Industry

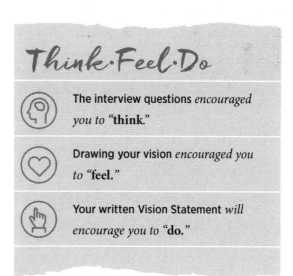

Think·Feel·Do

The interview questions *encouraged you to* **"think."**

Drawing your vision *encouraged you to* **"feel."**

Your written Vision Statement *will encourage you to* **"do."**

⚓ WHAT TO DO: Draft your Vision Statement in the space below. Refer to the real examples on the previous page for ideas.

My Personal Vision Statement

_____

_____

_____

_____

_____

_____

_____

_____

_____

_____

VISION WRAP-UP, REFLECTION & PRACTICE

I hope that once you got rolling, you found these Experiences fun and engaging. I encourage you to look at your work again tomorrow, next week and the week after.

This Experience stirs up a lot, and some people have told me they revisited their answers three times over the course of a few weeks or months. Each look is a new lens, so I invite you to return to these questions and your answers again and again.

Here's the main thing: You look to your VISION to guide your career choices. When the work you do today aligns with your VISION, the job or project means more. When you are more fully aware of what you want from your life and how work fits in, opportunities open. Instead of passively responding to whatever opportunities come along (like Mary, the global telecommunications director in the Introduction), even great ones offered by organizations' leaders, you enable yourself to seek, create or accept the projects, roles or jobs that resonate with your VIEW. You empower yourself to take charge.

Practice Box>

Commit to One Daily VISION

A practice is something you do every day with the intention to improve: They are simple and brief.[15] My goal is to help you acquire new habits so your new insights and skills stick with you and become part of your life. Here is the practice for you to implement for the next seven days:

➤ *Each morning, set a timer for one minute. Clear your mind of your to-do list. Use the minute to set one intention for the day, to do one small thing that helps you move toward your VISION.*

Next Week: INSIGHT

Insight

INSIGHT is self-awareness of who you are at your best

and worst, and your impact on others. This includes your

values, personal qualities and Signature Skills, both as you

understand them and as others experience them in you.

With true INSIGHT, you bring more of your Best Self to the

world and know what you want to change or improve upon

in service of living your VISION.

Insight

FEATURED EXPERIENCES:

④ Your Best Self

⑤ Your Signature Skills

⑥ Your Mirror

INSIGHT Wrap-Up, Reflection and Practice

WHO ARE YOU WHEN YOU ARE YOUR BEST SELF? How do others experience you? What do you enjoy doing? Where do you add value? When you are grounded in who you want to be, what you want to do, and how others experience you, you have INSIGHT.

Steve, a U.S. military officer whose role had shifted from the battlefield to an office job in Washington, D.C., arrived one spring at a business school in Greater Boston, Massachusetts, to be part of an executive education program. He then became a coaching client of mine. Before our third coaching conversation, I reviewed the results of two reports—a 360-feedback summary of people's perceptions of his strengths and weaknesses and Steve's self-assessment of his leadership style. The findings astonished me: There was an obvious misalignment between the people-oriented demands of his current job and the kind of job Steve's assessment predicted he would most enjoy—work where he could focus in a quiet environment with minimal interruptions. Although he enjoyed working with a team, too many conversations and meetings throughout the day sapped his energy. Like me, you might have expected his 360 raters to say that he had his door closed too often or that he didn't communicate with his people enough. But his boss, peers and direct reports said he was the best leader they had ever worked with! I couldn't wait to talk with Steve. How was he making the situation work?

Steve told me he knew from an early age he wanted to serve in the military, to protect people from harm and to foster peace. He'd lived this vision on battlefields and in the halls of the Pentagon. But in the early years of his career, Steve read a 360-feedback report that shocked him. His direct reports, colleagues and boss said they experienced him as a distant leader who prioritized doing tasks over building relationships. The feedback stung! However much he enjoyed problem solving, Steve knew that people, not tasks, made his work meaningful and he decided to do something about it.

Steve developed practices, actions he took every day to help change his behavior. For example, he paused at the start of a meeting to check in with people and ask how they were doing. He stopped in the middle of a task if he thought he could help someone improve a skill by providing in-the-moment coaching to a direct report or peer. And he protected time on his calendar to focus on solo tasks and enjoy the quiet he craves.

I love Steve's story because it shows that when you are strengthened with INSIGHT about your skills, qualities and values—both as you understand them and as others experience them—you can be successful at anything. It shows how Steve reflected on his experience, recognized his feelings about people's feedback and put practices into action to become the kind of leader he wanted to be.

This week, you will discover your Signature Skills, as well as blind spots that may be holding you back. You will:

Think·Feel·Do

 Define your "Best Self." *What do you want to be known for in your work life? What is your "Best Self"? The Experience will make you* **think**.

 Your Signature Skills. *Your Signature Skills are unique to you, strengths you enjoy using. This Experience will help you discover which skills give you joy and encourage you to* **feel**.

 Get Feedforward. *This week, you will seek the perspective of three people who can give you feedforward, an idea created by leadership guru Marshall Goldsmith. With feedforward, people offer their suggestions for how you can improve in the future. The Experiences will enable you to* **do** *something with your INSIGHT*

Outcomes for this week:	Why?
☐ *A written statement of your "Best Self" at work.*	You act with greater confidence when you are grounded in your Best Self.
☐ *An inventory of the skills that you are good at and enjoy using, as well as the skills you want to develop.*	Researchers have found that versatility differentiates high performers. With self-awareness, you strengthen your versatility, the ability to acquire new skills so you can adjust your behavior or approach to different people and situations.
☐ *360 feedback that provides a mirror and reflects how you are using your strengths and how others experience them; as well as feedforward, which includes suggestions for future change.*	Your strengths got you here but may not help you get to what's next. Feedback and feedforward will help you have a picture of the skills you may be over- or underusing.

TIP > "IT'S POLITICAL AROUND HERE."

Often, when people tell me they've hit a barrier because of organizational "politics," they are talking about the fairness of things. They believe that some people suck up to decision makers and get the best work assignments, or credit for things they don't deserve in return.

Life isn't always fair. There is little question that some playing fields are more level than others. Maybe you believe that the dynamics with specific people, your workplace, industry or the field in which you work, are especially unfair. There are too many reasons to name in this "tip box" for why you may be right, such as unconscious bias, or unintentional but real discrimination.

At the same time, as a coach, I've found that one reason some people seem to get all the attention and "good assignments" is because they have built other people's confidence in their capabilities.

There may be steps you could take to boost people's confidence in you. If you're feeling this way right now, as you work your way through this week's Experiences, consider opportunities you may have missed to present your Best Self, or use your Signature Skills to your advantage and to the benefit of your colleagues, clients or workplace.

INSIGHT EXPERIENCE #4: YOUR BEST SELF
Time: 15–30 mins.

Think of a time when you felt you were bringing your Best Self to work, when you fully tapped in to the qualities that are special to you and make you shine. Your Best Self means "being true to self. It means pursuing our full potential" and "being extraordinary," says researcher Robert Quinn and his colleagues.[16] How can you bring more of your Best Self to your work each day? Your personal definition of career success and satisfaction is the result of three things:

» *What you do (the job, projects and tasks, your performance, security, and contributing to the organization);*

» *The environment you work in (your networks, work/life balance, making a difference) and*

» *How you feel about your work (your sense of accomplishment, learning and self-development).*[17]

TO PREPARE FOR THIS EXPERIENCE:

> Have a timer handy.

> Download the Your Best-Self Card set at www.priorconsulting.com.

> Use a scissors to cut the cards from the printed sheets.

> If you can't download the cards or don't have time, you'll find an alternate Experience in the Resource Guide at the back of this book.

With a clear-eyed picture of your Best Self at work, you do the things that are authentically yours to do and define accomplishment by your own measures of success. When you bring your Best Self to work, you may also improve your "emotions, resistance to disease, resilience to stress and burnout, creative problem solving, performance under pressure and relationships with [your] employer," says researcher Daniel Cable and his colleagues.[18]

In her book *Presence*, Amy Cuddy, Harvard faculty and TED-Talks guru, makes a convincing case for this idea. She argues that when you are in tune with what you stand for and what you care about, you increase your personal power and approach situations with greater confidence. "Beyond improving confidence and performance on specific tasks, knowing who we are can also elevate our sense of meaning in life," Cuddy says.[19]

∿ **WHAT TO DO:** What is *your* Best Self? What qualities do you want to be known for in the world? As a coach, I see that the people who are most happy in their work find a way to deliver what's needed while being true to who they are. Don't get me wrong, you can't live each of your best qualities 100 percent of the time. If your Best Self is fun-loving and fancy-free, you know that there is a time and place for those qualities in any work situation. At the same time, if fun is essential to who you are and you work in a place or an industry where no one ever cracks a smile, you're bound to feel less happy in your work over time.

So, to be clear, as you do this Experience, consider your Best Self as your *whole* self.

Here's the main idea: You will have five minutes to select 16 cards from a deck of 80, each printed with a specific quality or trait. The cards you choose will resonate with your vision of your Best Self. You'll organize the cards into a diamond shape, and then take a photo so you have it to refer to later.

> ➤ *Keep in mind that the cards you pull will represent an aspiration/desire/wish of your vision for your Best Self. You may or may not be living this version of yourself today.*

Finally, don't be alarmed by the five-minute rule. Trust me, five minutes is just the right amount of time.

Discover Your Best-Self

1. Assemble what you need before you begin. Please see the box on the previous page for preparations.

2. Your gut is your guidance system. The sort should be a flow, where you instinctively react to each word. Work quickly. This is the reason for the five-minute timer, to help you avoid overthinking.

3. Read the following directions before you begin, so you know where you are heading.

4. Set a timer to five minutes.

5. Start the timer and begin to sort the cards.

6. Flip through the cards and sort them into two piles. One pile consists of adjectives that you can quickly reject. The other pile consists of cards that you have a gut feeling about and make you say "yes," that grab you and sound like something you'd like to be as part of your Best Self.

7.   Pare the "yes" pile down to 16 cards.

8.   Arrange the cards into a diamond shape.

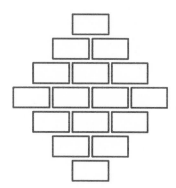

The word that resonates most strongly for you will be the one on top.
This is the most important quality you want to be known for, your
vision of your Best Self. The next line will have the two second-most-
important qualities, then three on the next line. The fourth line will have
four cards, then three, then two, then one, a quality that is important
but is not quite as meaningful as the others.

9.   Take a snapshot of your diamond. You will come back to this in
      Week 4: WILL.

❧ WHAT TO DO:

1. When your diamond is complete and you've taken a snapshot, review your cards.

2. What patterns do you notice? For example, did you choose cardswith similar meanings, such as kind, compassion, caring? Trustworthy,ethical, honest? Diligent, disciplined, careful? Trail-blazer, innovative,creative?

3. Consolidate which cards seem similar to you. What's the main theme about your Best Self?

4. Write your Best-Self Statement using the template below.

_____

_____

_____

Here is a few real examples:

Wei was a rising leader and technical manager in an online retail company. She completed this Experience as part of a coaching conversation. She sorted through 81 cards, each with one adjective, and selected 16 qualities that added up to a vision of her Best Self that she didn't feel she was living today. Then, Wei drafted an aspirational statement: **I want to be known as an empathetic, creative and adaptable manager, which would enable me to achieve better results for the organization and be a better coach and mentor to my people.** *Soon after Wei and I began our work together, the organization restructured and downsized. Wei felt she was constantly pulled away from the work she had planned for the day and into emergency meetings instead. Months later, in a follow-up coaching session, we revisited her Best-Self aspirations.*

"What progress are you making in living your Best Self?" I asked.

"Honestly, Lisa, I haven't looked at my statement since I wrote it three months ago. It's just been too busy," Wei confessed.

So we dusted off her VISION worksheet and compared where she was three months earlier to where she was today. When she reread her Best-Self Statement, Wei was amazed. Even though she'd forgotten about the writing the words, she'd made tangible progress in bringing her Best Self to life.

How could this be true?

First, instead of just daydreaming about her Best Self, she wrote it down, so the picture was more concrete and real. Second, I asked Wei to identify one daily "practice," an action that she could do every day with the intention to achieve her Best Self. For her practice, Wei chose to begin each day by identifying at least one task or project she could delegate effectively to one of her team members. This helped Wei in two ways: She spent less time doing the tasks herself and more time building the skills of people on her team. She saved time, and her people grew in their jobs. The team's overall performance improved. Wei didn't need to revisit the written statement because she was living her Best Self every day through her practice.

How is this relevant to me?

Two ways! First, by writing your Best-Self Statement, the idea will stick with you, even if you don't return to it until I ask you to in the upcoming weeks. Second, like Wei, at the end of this week, you're going to identify a practice that enables you to be your Best Self.

INSIGHT EXPERIENCE #5: YOUR SIGNATURE SKILLS
Time: 15–30 mins.

What are your unique Signature Skills, those talents or ways of working with people that are part of your Best Self, that differentiate you from others?

Playing to your strengths boosts your mood and self-esteem, which leads to greater work satisfaction, according to research by famed psychologist Martin Seligman, a founder of the field of Positive Psychology. Strengths-based career counseling led to more people finding jobs than did traditional approaches that focused on improving weaknesses, as other studies have found.[20] The exercise starting on the next page helps you hone your Signature Skills.

No one will see this but you, so be honest with yourself. Next week, you will ask for feedback and feedforward from people who know you. For now, this is your self-assessment.

✒ WHAT TO DO:

1. **Review the list of skills on the next few pages.** For each skill, answer the assessment questions. If there is a skill you score with a low level of proficiency but you believe you should further develop, check the Develop column.

2. **You will use these Skills Assessment results in later activities.** You may also decide later to revise which skills you check to Develop.

Example:

Qualities and Skills	Enter 1-5 for Level of Proficiency	Enjoy Using?	Yes / No Develop? Check if yes
Allocating Time and Energy Effectively	4	Yes	
Approachability	3	No	√
Teamwork	3	No	
Technical Skills	5	Yes	√

There's a built-in bias to say you enjoy skills that may be required for success in your work today: You may be tempted to fudge your results. Be honest. In the example above, the person is great at technical work but doesn't enjoy working in teams. Perhaps working with people drains her energy. But there is hope! She could use her strengths to overcome the situation. For example, she could hold team meetings to teach a technical skill, or support people in the group mentoring and coaching one another.

Qualities and Skills	Enter 1-5 for Level of Proficiency	Enjoy Using?	Yes / No Develop? Check if yes
Allocating Time and Energy Effectively			
Approachability			
Asking Effective Questions			
Boss Relationships			
Building Effective Teams			
Business Knowledge and Savvy			
Change Management			
Coaching Skills			
Coalition Building			
Collaboration			
Comfort Around Senior Leaders			
Comfort with Ambiguity			
Compassion			
Composure			
Confidence			
Conflict Management			

Qualities and Skills	Enter 1-5 for Level of Proficiency	Enjoy Using?	Yes / No Develop? Check if yes
Courage			
Creativity			
Cross-Cultural Communication			
Customer Focus			
Client Relationships			
Confronting Issues			
Critical Thinking			
Decision Making			
Delegation			
Developing Others			
Directing People or Work			
Emotional/Social Intelligence			
Energy/Passion			
Ethics			
Fairness to Others			
Forgiveness			
Functional/Technical Skills			
Goal Oriented			
Hiring			
Honesty			
Humility			

Qualities and Skills	Enter 1-5 for Level of Proficiency	Enjoy Using?	Yes / No Develop? Check if yes
Informing			
Innovation			
Integrity			
Interpersonal Sensitivity			
Judgment			
Leadership			
Listening			
Love of Learning			
Managing Diversity			
Managing Work and			
Measuring Outcomes			
Mindfulness			
Motivating Others			
Negotiating			
Organizing			
Ownership and Accountability			
Patience			
Peer Relationships			
Perseverance			
Perspective			
Planning			

Qualities and Skills	Enter 1-5 for Level of Proficiency	Enjoy Using?	Yes / No Develop? Check if yes
Political Savvy			
Presence			
Presentation Skills/Public Speaking			
Problem Solving			
Process Oriented			
Productivity			
Quality Oriented			
Responsive			
Results Oriented			
Scanning the Horizon			
Self-Awareness			
Self-Development			
Self-Regulation			
Sense of Humor			
Systems Oriented			
Teamwork			
Transparency			
Understanding Others			
Verbal Communications			
Work/Life Balance			
Written Communications			

Other (fill in)			

> **WHAT TO DO:** Refer to the assessment you completed above. Write your answers in the corresponding space on the right.

Which skills . . .	Responses and Reflections
are you most proficient in, and enjoy using the most? *Write them here. If you use these strengths every day, you are finding greater satisfaction in your job. People may come to you as the "go-to" person because your energy, experience and knowledge invite them to approach you for information, guidance or mentoring. Your engagement is so apparent that it energizes and engages others.* > *These are qualities and skills you want to* **use more.**	
are you most proficient in, but enjoy using the least? *If you are using these every day but not enjoying them, you may be heading for burnout or becoming "unconsciously incompetent" at executing these tasks. Your dissatisfaction may become so great that you make mistakes more frequently or appear to others as if you don't care.* > *These are qualities and skills you want to* **use less.**	

do you underuse or want to develop, for your own career satisfaction or in service of your VISION?

These qualities and skills are emerging areas of interest or expertise. For example, a technical expert who needs to build influence skills, or a manager who needs to spend less energy producing and more effort developing the team, or someone in an early-stage career who wants to build confidence and a reputation.

> *These are qualities and skills you want to develop.*

What Happens Next?

Let's step back for a moment to look at the Experiences you've completed, how they fit together and where we're heading next. In Week 1, you created a VISION. This week, you are gaining INSIGHT. In your first Experience, you defined your Best Self. In the second Experience, you identified your Signature Skills. But wait. Before we move on to the final INSIGHT Experience . . .

We Interrupt Our Regular Program for an Author Confession

I am not entirely on board with the "focus only on your strengths" bandwagon. Research shows that areas for improvement matter too. "You can take strengths too far," say assessment experts Robert E. Kaplan and Robert B. Kaiser.[21] Your strengths can become your weaknesses. I'll use an analogy from my son's years as an athlete to explain.

Ben was a serious, high school track and field athlete who relied on his physical strength to power through a long jump or sprint. During freshman-year practices, he used his strength to keep up with state champions, even though he hadn't had the same level of preparation. When I pointed this out to my teenage son, he insisted he was "fine" and continued to push. By the end of sophomore year, I was driving Ben to physical therapy twice a week.

"Everything pulls on everything," the physical therapist told Ben. He'd overused his strong quadriceps, the large leg muscles in front, which weakened the back hamstrings. As his performance declined, Ben despaired. Eventually, he realized he needed to create new practices, actions to take every day to return to health and prevent future injury, such as doing specific exercises to shore up weaker muscles. During his senior year, he achieved his goals and learned not to over-rely on his strengths.

I've seen this dynamic of overusing strengths play out in the workplace as well. Sean was a senior human resources manager at a medical device organization where I was consulting on a project. In a casual conversation one day, Sean told me he'd been reading about Signature Strengths. Inspired by gurus of the movement, Sean told me, "I'm not going to focus on my weaknesses. From now on, I am going to play to my strengths." The problem: His job required him to deliver on the tasks that he didn't enjoy or do well. His strengths were building relationships and facilitating team meetings. His much-lesser strengths were generating Excel spreadsheets and managing payroll. Over time, Sean prioritized too much time facilitating workshops and spent so much time building relationships that his managers and colleagues thought he was schmoozing or wasting time. His weaknesses compromised his effectiveness, but he insisted on his "strengths-only" strategy. When Sean left the organization and went to work at another firm, the next job ended in the same dissatisfying way. Blind to how he over-relied on his strengths, he brought the problem from workplace to workplace.

INSIGHT EXPERIENCE #6: YOUR MIRROR
Time: Three 30 minute conversations, plus prep

In this experience, you will compare your self-perceptions of Best Self and Signature Skills with the perceptions of others by finding three people whom you trust and asking them for *feedforward,* as introduced by author Marshall Goldsmith.

Feedforward is being open to others' ideas or advice for how you can be successful in the future. Athletic coaches have used feedforward techniques for decades to help their athletes visualize a great performance—clearing a personal record in the high jump in track and field, or executing a perfect triple axel in figure skating. Swim coaches found that when children were encouraged to visualize themselves doing swim strokes they had not even been taught, their swimming skills improved significantly.[22] The coaches' suggestions and advice for how to be successful in the future propelled the athletes to improve.

Not everyone feels comfortable asking for other people's opinions about our strengths, weaknesses or how we are doing. Some workplaces encourage these kinds of conversations, while others avoid them. This means that some of the people you ask for feedforward may find your request odd. Don't worry; the blueprint is here for making this a productive learning experience. Consider this essential to creating your VIEW.

You're making this sound like I should eat my spinach. Why is it useful?
"People are terrible at estimating their abilities," says Carol Dweck, author of *Mindset.* You can't observe yourself as you go through your day. What do other people value in you that you were not even aware of? Do you over-rely on your strengths? Do you know about your blind spots? How might you be getting in your own way when it comes to moving toward your VIEW? In this Experience, you'll seek feedforward about your Best Self and Signature Skills so you can stop guessing and start learning.

So what does this idea look like in action?
Early in my career, I worked in the human resources department of a company that helped create the Internet. I was responsible for sorting through hundreds of performance reviews to identify common development needs so we could offer relevant employee training classes. Shuffling through a stack one day, I was startled by the stark review that

one company president wrote for a director who reported to him. He had penned two words in thick red ink, three-inches tall:

"Great guy."

That was it. The form was two pages long. It looked naked except for those two words. The higher people go in an organization, the less feedback they receive, which is ironic because the stakes get higher for both the organization and the person who has increasing responsibility and complexity. What made the leader "great"? What should he keep doing or do differently? Where was the specificity?

Today, as an executive coach, it's part of my job to help people get the specific suggestions for improvement they need so they can be more effective. At one professional services firm, I helped Joshua, a new manager, think about how to frame key messages he wanted to deliver to Cheryl, one of his direct reports, in a performance review. He drafted a statement before our meeting. "Cheryl needs to improve her innovation," he wrote. What did that mean? What could Cheryl do with that kind of suggestion? Just like the senior leader who got the message "Great guy," the suggestion wasn't specific. It didn't offer ideas for the future for how to improve.

How do these stories relate to me?

You are about to ask people for feedforward, for their perspective on strengths you use or underuse as well as suggestions for future improvement. If someone says, "You're great!!" take the compliment. Let the praise sink in. Then, ask for more specifics:

› *Can you tell me about a time when you saw me using that strength? Overusing?*

› *What impact does this strength have on other people?*

› *What other strengths could I be using?*

This isn't a performance review or a scripted process. It's a chance to ask your own questions so you know how close you are to *living* your Best Self and using your Signature Skills every day. Does your work encourage the best of yourself? This experience exercises your feedforward muscles. Over time, this becomes second nature and feeds your entire VIEW.

One last story before you go out and get your personalized feedforward. I remember this scene like it was yesterday. One day, when I was in high school, I was shopping in a department store with my friend Sarah. She picked up a pair of shoes from a display. "Do you like these shoes?" she asked. I knew Sarah's fashion tastes to be simple but elegant. I didn't think the shoes were the best choice for her.

"Hmmm, no, not really," I said as I picked up one of the shoes and turned it over. Sarah explained why she thought the shoes were terrific. So I got more specific. "I've never seen you wear this shoe color and the shoes don't really fit your style," I said. Sarah then insisted on offering three more reasons why I should see things her way. Her reasoning didn't change my mind, but I confess I started to feel annoyed. Why ask my opinion if there was only one acceptable answer?

That's when it hit me: Sometimes a person can ask for our opinion but not want to hear an answer that contradicts with the way they see things. Sometimes, people ask for our perspective when they just want us to validate their choices and behaviors.

Like Sarah, do you ever ask for someone's opinion, only to argue with their answer if it conflicts with the way that you see things?

Over the years, I've witnessed firsthand how people can struggle with perspectives that contradict with how they see themselves. Sometimes, the first response is denial.

Susan, a midlevel corporate manager in a hedge-fund company, looked up from her feedback report. We had used an online 360 approach, where raters assess a manager's skill on a scale of one to five. A "one" indicated an area for improvement; "five" indicated a strength. We weren't really looking for high or low scores. We were looking for trends. The trend on Susan's report: lots of room for improvement.

"Something is wrong with this report," Susan said earnestly. "Your instructions weren't clear, so the raters misunderstood the scale and got it backwards." I knew that raters had written very specific examples in the comments section of the survey to support their ratings. I felt sad for her. Her self-perceptions were so far out of alignment with the people she worked with that her first reaction to feedback was to say that something was wrong with both the tool and her raters.

The moral of these stories: The people who care about you the most will give you the gift of their authentic perspective. They want you to succeed and they can often see the skills you're over- and underusing in ways that you cannot. It may not be easy to hear when someone who cares says that you could choose a better pair of shoes or be more patient with colleagues who lack your IT skills, but be grateful for the person's courage and heart.

In her research, Carol Dweck found that people with a fixed mindset, like Susan, are less likely to be open to other people's perspectives on their performance if that perspective conflicts with their own. With a more open, growth-focused mindset, you can better receive suggestions for future improvement.[23] Learn how to maintain an open mind. Choose stakeholders who will give you an honest and varied perspective.

Who are my stakeholders?

Stakeholders are the people who rely on your performance for their own work success or personal growth and satisfaction. Stakeholders are also the people who can block you from getting what you want, as my friend Eileen, former HR executive of a large global financial services firm, once told me. Stakeholders can include your family, friends, clients, colleagues and boss. As you go through this Experience, don't stack the deck with people who are going to tell you how amazing you are! Identify at least one person with whom this might be a difficult conversation. Also, try to have a variety of people who see you in different situations.

❧ **WHAT TO DO:** Choose three people whom you will contact and schedule time with to ask for feedforward. Because of scheduling constraints, it may take a few weeks to get on their calendar. If you can't have all three conversations this week, continue working through the upcoming Experiences at your current pace. You can always come back to the Experiences, which I encourage you to do even when you've completed your six weeks. For now, do what you need to maintain your momentum!

1. Identify your stakeholders.

Choose three people whose opinions you value and who have experienced you in enough situations to provide input and advice.

Example List

Person	How this person knows me (Manager, Colleague, Direct Report, Family Member, etc.)
Warren Peace	Colleague, works with me on Alpha project
Mary Littlelamb	My manager
Pat Smith	Spouse/Partner

Your List

Person	How this person knows me (Manager, Colleague, Direct Report, Family Member, etc.)

Write your stakeholder names and their relationship to you in the spaces below.

1	
2	
3	

2. Schedule the three conversations.

Describe your request and schedule 45 minutes of conversation. Treat the person to coffee or lunch, or set up a conversation over Skype. Please don't have the conversation over email.

> *Suggested wording for your email or phone call to schedule time:*

"I am doing some career development work and I'd value your input on what you see me doing well and what you think I could do differently. Can I treat you to coffee or lunch and set up some time? We'd need about 45 minutes to an hour. Don't worry, you won't hurt my feelings if you have something difficult to tell me. I'm trying to gain more insight about my strengths and how other people experience me. I trust you and would benefit from your perspective. Here are examples of questions I'd like to discuss: When have you seen me at my best? What was I doing?

» *What strengths could I continue to develop and improve upon?*

» *Which strengths do I over-rely on?*

» *What advice do you have for me going forward?*

Here are some dates I'm available. Please let me know what works for you, or suggest other times. Many thanks in advance for your time and support!"

3. Before the conversation.

> *Review the templates and advice on the next few pages. This includes questions for you to ask during the discussion. Add or revise according to your own situation.*

> *Confirm the time and location with the person; ask if they have any questions or suggestions for the conversation.*

4. During the conversation.

▸ *Use the "Your Mirror" templates on the next three pages, one for each person.* *To make this as easy as possible for you, each template includes the questions you will ask.*

▸ *Take charge of your fight-freeze-flight response. Even though we live in a world of Careers 3.0, we can have a primal response to perceived danger. While humans never actually existed at the time of the T-Rex, parts of our brains are built for the dinosaur age. Under threat, the almond-sized amygdala back near the brainstem triggers the urge to fight, freeze or flee. If you hear answers you don't like in response to your questions for feedforward, your "dinosaur brain," a term first coined by authors Albert J. Bernstein and Sydney C. Rozen, may get fired up.*[24]

▸ *Be aware of your physical response. When it senses danger, your body produces cortisol, the stress hormone that provokes a physical reaction. You may sweat, blush or fidget. To counteract:*

» *Breathe deeply. Inhale through your nose. Hold for four counts. Exhale for four counts. Repeat as needed.*

» *Ask questions. This will help put you in listening mode. Active listening is the process of staying focused in the moment and being open to learning. "What I hear you saying is . . ." "Would you please clarify . . ." "How did that make people feel?" "What could I have done differently?"*

» *Recognize your triggers. Your physical response to "danger" can trigger an emotional response. Paying attention to how you feel is a practical matter. Your emotions can hijack an otherwise productive conversation. There are different kinds of triggers. One is when your perception of the facts is quite different from the person's, like our example with Susan, who thought something was wrong with the report and the raters.*[25] *Your relationship with the person could trigger an emotional response, for example, if you don't trust the person, you may feel less safe hearing feedforward. Or, like in the example with my friend Sarah, who just wanted me to agree with her opinion, you may just expect your good friend to tell you great things about yourself. Your vision of your Best Self can also be a trigger. For example, if you believe your Best Self is innovative, but someone gives feedback on how you could be bringing more new ideas to a project, that feedback could feel like an attack on your self-identity. Take note of your reaction, remain composed and choose your response.*

5. After the conversation, Thank the person.

Follow up with a written note, either handwritten, by text or email, depending on the person and your relationship.

Think of these five steps as a gentle breeze at your back, a supportive tailwind. The goal here is to make it a little easier for you to get the INSIGHT you need so you can make the most of your unique talents and create the life and work you envision.

What if I have an introverted energy and find it challenging to reach out to people? Asking for feedforward can be challenging for anyone, but perhaps especially so for people who don't like to be the center of attention, are more quiet or have introverted energy. As Susan Cain, author of the best-selling book Quiet: *The Power of Introverts in a World That Can't Stop Talking*, says, "Highly sensitive people also process information about their environments—both physical and emotional—unusually deeply."[26] If this is true for you, then make this process your own. Adjust the steps; do what you need to make the experience right for you.

"The secret to life is to put yourself in the right lighting. For some it's a Broadway spotlight; for others, a lamplit desk. Use your natural powers—of persistence, concentration, insight, and sensitivity—to do work you love and work that matters. Solve problems, make art, think deeply."

— Susan Cain, author of *Quiet: The Power of Introverts in a World That Can't Stop Talking*

✤ **WHAT TO DO: Use these suggested questions as a template for your Feedforward**

Conversation with Person 1.

Person's Name:	
Relationship to You:	
Questions:	» What should I continue doing? For example, When have you seen me at my best? What skills or qualities did I demonstrate?
	_____
	_____
	_____
	» What should I stop doing? For example, which strengths do I overuse?
	_____
	_____
	_____
	» What should I start doing? For example, what could I continue to develop and improve upon?
	_____
	_____
	_____
	» Is there anything else?
	_____
	_____
	_____
	» Say thank you!

๑ **WHAT TO DO:** Use these suggested questions as a template for your Feedforward

Conversation with Person 2.

Person's Name:	
Relationship to You:	
Questions:	» What should I continue doing? For example, When have you seen me at my best? What skills or qualities did I demonstrate? ——————————— ——————————— ——————————— » What should I stop doing? For example, which strengths do I overuse? ——————————— ——————————— ——————————— » What should I start doing? For example, what could I continue to develop and improve upon? ——————————— ——————————— ——————————— » Is there anything else? ——————————— ——————————— ——————————— » Say thank you!

✍ **WHAT TO DO: Use these suggested questions as a template for your Feedforward**

Conversation with Person 3.

Person's Name:	
Relationship to You:	
Questions:	» What should I continue doing? For example, When have you seen me at my best? What skills or qualities did I demonstrate? _____ _____ _____ » What should I stop doing? For example, which strengths do I overuse? _____ _____ _____ » What should I start doing? For example, what could I continue to develop and improve upon? _____ _____ _____ » Is there anything else? _____ _____ _____ » Say thank you!

Reflection: What's Your Secret Sauce?

✎ WHAT TO DO: What did you learn from your feedforward conversations? Write your answers to the questions below:

> *What is unique about you? What are the key ingredients of your "secret sauce," the Signature Skills and personal qualities that differentiate you from other people and make you special?*

_____

_____

_____

_____

_____

_____

_____

> *What strengths are you over-or under-using? Write about them here.*

_____

_____

_____

_____

_____

_____

_____

Your Action Plan

Use the template below to write an Action Plan based on your INSIGHT from this week. Below is an example.

Example

In the example below, the person wants to continue developing his Signature Skill and wants to stop over-relying on it. In other words, he wants to use his Signature Skill more effectively and intentionally.

The Signature Skills *I want to . . .*		Goal and Action	Time Frame	Resources/ Someone who can help
Use more or develop. What's my secret sauce?	*Getting people's input on a project.*	*My goal is to be more self-aware of when I am using this strength.* *Action: I will be even more intentional about when and why I am asking for input.*	*I can begin now. This is something I can do every day.*	*I can ask project team members for frequent feedback on how I am including different points of view.*
Use less because I'm overusing and/or this is a blind spot.	*Getting people's input on a project!*	*My goal is to be more effective using this skill.* *Action: Learn more about influence skills so I have more tools for knowing when to get the right amount of input and when to stop.*	*I can begin now. Again, it's something I can do every day.*	*Find a good book on influence skills.* *Ask my manager for more frequent feedback.*

INSIGHT WRAP-UP, REFLECTION AND PRACTICE

Your Action Plan

> *What did you learn from this week's Experiences? Use this template to turn your INSIGHT into action.*

The Signature Skills *I want to* . . .	Goal and Action	Time Frame	Resources/ Someone who can help
Use more or develop. What's my secret sauce?			
Use less because I'm overusing and/or this is a blind spot.			

Practice Box>

Commit to One Daily INSIGHT Practice

A practice is something you do every day with the intention to improve.[27] Here's your practice for the next seven days:

> *Choose one skill or trait you would like to improve and assess your progress every day. Research shows that if you are already using your strongest strengths effectively, you will benefit most by focusing on those strengths you could improve.[28] At the end of every day, take one minute to ask yourself, "What did I do to improve this skill or trait? What is one thing I could have done differently?"*

Next Week: ENGAGEMENT

PART II

ENGAGEMENT & WILL

Practice & Act

ENGAGEMENT

is your skill in creating work opportunities that are both

meaningful to you and aligned with the purpose and goals

of something you are part of, whether you work for an

organization or for yourself. You take charge of creating

this sweet spot—what I call the NeXus—where your VIEW

intersects with the VIEW of an organization, customer or

client. The greater the overlap in the NeXus, the more fully

engaged, energized and absorbed you feel, a state of mind

known as *flow.*

ENGAGEMENT

FEATURED EXPERIENCES:

(7) **Your Work Aspiration**

(8) **Your Organization's VIEW**

(9) **Your NeXtivity**

Wrap-Up, Reflection and Practice

WHAT IF YOU HAD THE POWER to deploy your professional passions in your job today—to create meaningful work opportunities that develop your skills and prepare you for what's next?

Maria, second-in-charge of a well-known nonprofit, wanted to step out as a leader. Her VISION was to create a new model for working with vulnerable women in Boston's urban communities. She gained INSIGHT through 360 feedback from her team, colleagues, her boss and civic leaders, who described her best qualities as a strong relationship builder with a great reputation among clients. They said that Maria's Signature Skills included marketing programs in the community, managing people and implementing programs that helped women transition from public assistance to work.

But Maria lacked key executive skills such as strategic planning and fundraising; this reality was holding her back. Her boss, reluctant to take a chance, assigned her the same old projects; the job lost its challenge. Getting out of bed with less enthusiasm for the workday ahead, Maria fretted about the future, felt stuck. She could never become head of this nonprofit as long as her manager was in the leading role; he'd made it clear he was there to stay. She felt she had two choices: learn new skills in her current job or leave for another nonprofit.

I saw a third way. Maria needed to answer three questions, which sum up the power of ENGAGEMENT:

How could she . . .

- find more "flow" in her current job, so she could reclaim her passion and the sense of challenge and accomplishment she once felt?

- provide a valuable service or outcome to the organization, so it could be even more successful in achieving its vision and goals?

- prepare for the future, so she could move toward what she envisioned next?

By answering these questions, Maria devised a win-win plan and had a heart-to-heart with her manager. Knowing that her manager needed to free up some of his own time to focus on legislative affairs that impacted the nonprofit, Maria proposed taking charge of some aspects of the organization's finances that consumed his time and energy, including preparing and delivering segments of board presentations. She also proposed playing a more active role in strengthening board member relationships, which would play to her Signature Skills while giving her the opportunity to participate in discussions about strategy. Her manager saw the win-win and they implemented the plan. With each step, she moved closer to her VISION for work and career. When an opportunity to be chief of a different organization came along, she was ready. Today, she's the executive director of a nationally recognized nonprofit.

We're not just talking about a job or a gig, we're talking about the work that is uniquely yours to do, the work that moves you toward your VISION; enables you to put your Best Self to work. You feel fully energized and absorbed in what you are doing and your employer benefits as well. It's a win-win.

This week, I'm going to coach you through these three questions just like I did for Maria. If you are self-employed, I'll offer tips for how you can apply the experiences to your work. And if you are between jobs, I'll offer tips for you as well.

Before we get there, I'd like to clarify a few terms.

I want to avoid any confusion that may arise with the word engagement. Many employers think about engagement as a measure of how willing employees are to give their extra time and energy to help the organization succeed. Data on engagement suggests that organizations that have highly engaged employees outperform their competitors in the marketplace. Although the idea is related, we're talking about something more personal, powerful and deep than a corporate buzzword.

ENGAGEMENT is your answer to Maria's three questions, your VISION and INSIGHT in action. You deploy more of your passions in your current situation so you can move toward what's next. You do this by creating the NeXus between your VIEW and the goals of your employer or clients.

Think·Feel·Do This week, to help you chart your personal path to greater ENGAGEMENT at work, you will:

 Write one work aspiration *for your current job for the next six months to one year. This week, you will focus intensively on your work life and take a deeper dive into what you want from your work experience, which will encourage you to* **think**.

 Find your NeXtivity. *This is where it all comes together, where you find development activities in the NeXus between your employer's VIEW and your own. You will identify one task, project or experience that you* **feel** *excited about and that prepares you for the future.*

 Consider your organization's needs *for the next six months to one year. What is the vision? What are the goals? What changes will impact the industry, organization or team? This Experience helps you identify things you can* **do.**

Outcomes for this week:

 Your VIEW: A written aspiration for your work life.

 Your organization's VIEW: A quick scan of the organization's needs.

 **Your NeXtivity:** A development opportunity you could pitch to your manager, client, or potential employer. (You'll get help with how to write your pitch in Week 5.)

Why?

Your current work experience may be a goldmine of opportunity for your professional development.

- To stay relevant in the workplace, keep a finger on the pulse of trends. How will your industry, organization, business, profession or job change?

- With your finger on the pulse, you are more prepared and resilient. This is essential for ongoing work-security, whether you are self-employed, a rising star in an organization or are content to simply do your best work in exchange for a paycheck.

- When you're prepared with a proposal for a development assignment and how it will benefit the team or organization, you'll increase your confidence and chances of success.

TIP >IF YOU ARE SELF-EMPLOYED:

You can think of your "Employer" in two different ways:

> You are your business. What does your "company" need to move to the next level?

> Your clients are your "employer," in the sense that they are paying you for a product or service. What are their needs, collectively or individually?

If you are between jobs: You can use the experiences as a blueprint to help you:

> Get clearer about what's important to you in your next role.

> Learn more about an organization or industry.

> Develop a pitch for volunteering your service, as a way of getting a foot in the door.

HELLO, NEXUS

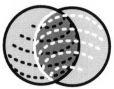 Whether you work for someone else or for yourself, you find the most satisfaction and joy when you create the work that fulfills your VIEW. It's a simple idea that's hard to do. It begins with targeting the NeXus, the win-win intersection between your VIEW and the goals of your organization. The bigger the NeXus, the greater the win-win.

OK, I get it. But where do I begin?

We'll walk through the questions that Maria answered so she could pinpoint the NeXus between her VIEW and the needs of her workplace. Through these Experiences you will explore how to:

- **find more "flow"** in your current job, so you can deploy your passion; find moremeaning and challenge.

- **provide a valuable service** or outcome to the organization, so it could be even moresuccessful in achieving its vision and goals.

- **prepare yourself for the future**, so you can master your Signature Skills or learn newones that move you toward what you want next.

ENGAGEMENT EXPERIENCE #7: YOUR WORK ASPIRATION
Time: 5–20 mins.

> *When do you feel flow at work?*

You keep talking about flow, what is it?

Flow is a state of mind where you are energized by and completely absorbed in what you are doing. You are engaged in the "optimal experience" of an activity "for its own sake."[29] The hours fly by, distractions fade to the background. Work boosts your energy. Famed psychologist Mihaly Csikszentmihalyi, Distinguished Professor of Psychology and Management at Claremont Graduate University coined the term through his studies on happiness. Through his research, he noted that more income or "increases in material resources [do] not increase happiness" and wondered what that was all about. As he began to study artists, musicians and scientists, people who invested their time and creativity without expecting superior financial rewards, he discovered people who were happy with their work life to the extent that doing the work for its own sake was the reward. Csikszentmihalyi and his researchers interviewed thousands of people from all over the world, from corporate employees to Himalayan mountain climbers. They collapsed all of their findings into a summary, adapted here for your convenience from Csikszentmihalyi's TED Talk:[30]

- **Completely involved** in what I am doing—focused, concentrated.

- **Great inner clarity**—knowing what needs to be done, and how well I am doing.

- **Knowing that the activity is doable**—that my skills are adequate to the task.

- **A sense of serenity**—no worries about myself, and a feeling of growing beyond my current role or skills.

- **Thoroughly focused** on the present, hours seem to pass by in minutes.

- **Inner motivation**—whatever produces flow becomes its own reward."[31]

Helpful. But I'm trying to understand, what does flow have to do with taking charge of my VIEW?

You experience flow when you are doing work that fuels your **VISION** and enables you to deepen INSIGHT so you are living your Best Self and using your Signature Skills. So, it has everything to do with your VIEW. The idea is to bring more flow into your job today, for your own benefit as well as for your employer or client.

In this Experience, you are going to write one aspirational goal for your development or increased flow in your work situation over the next six to 12 months. If you are self-employed, you can think of your answer in the context of the projects or your business in general. If you are between jobs, this is a chance to be more specific about naming the situation you want to move toward.

Now that you understand what flow is, pause for a moment to reflect and write your answer to this question: when do you feel flow at work?

_____

_____

_____

ക് **WHAT TO DO** : Write a work goal so you can take a step forward in creating the career of your dreamsor simply enjoy today's work experience even more. Here are just a few example goals:

- Find more flow in my current work situation

- Learn a new skill or deepen my expertise in a particular area based on INSIGHTS from Week 2

- Make a career change

- Expand my job responsibilities or earn a promotion

- Improve my performance in my current role

- Learn about another department or profession

1. Your View

Draft one aspirational goal for your work life the next six months to
one year.

Keep it simple. For a great list of ideas, check out the many examples for
goal setting on in the Resources Section at the back of the book. Choose one or two from
the list or find inspiration to draft your own.

_____

_____

_____

_____

_____

_____

_____

_____

_____

_____

_____

_____

_____

_____

_____

_____

ENGAGEMENT EXPERIENCE #8:
YOUR ORGANIZATION'S VIEW
Time: 15–30 mins.

Your career success relies on your ability to contribute something valuable to the success of other people and your organization. To do this, you need to understand your organization's VIEW. Organizations are living things that transition through stages of development, like people—from start-up to maturity to decline to renewal. Just like people, organizations learn; the process is remarkably like the stages of adult learning, as my own research proposed.[32]

HERE'S MY TAKE ON "ORGANIZATION'S VIEW":

- **An organization's VISION** is an inspiring picture of what the leaders want to accomplish. In the best organizations, you feel engaged by the vision: cure cancer; create a better financial future for stakeholders; solve wicked social issues; educate future leaders; colonize space.

- **INSIGHT is when leaders understand** what the organization does best. Leaders seek feedback from customers, investors and employees and use it to improve products, services, sales, operations and the work environment.

- **ENGAGEMENT.** By understanding trends in the marketplace, organizations createthe best products and services that meet theNeXus between the leaders' vision and needs of customers, employees, shareholders, partners and suppliers.

- **WILL.** The lifecycle of companies is shrinking. In aworld of 3.0, products and services fade toirrelevance in the blink of an eye. To survive,senior leaders must make choices.

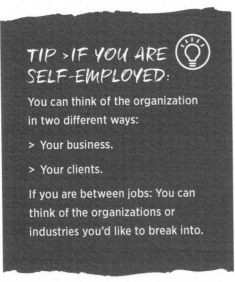

TIP >IF YOU ARE SELF-EMPLOYED:

You can think of the organization in two different ways:

> Your business.

> Your clients.

If you are between jobs: You can think of the organizations or industries you'd like to break into.

OK, I get it. But how can I learn about the organization's VIEW?

Here is a secret from the executive suite: successful senior leaders have the ability to "scan the horizon." They step back to see the big picture, such as where the organization is going and the outside forces and trends that will impact success. I think that everyone needs to have this skill in order to add value and stay relevant in the workplace.

I think that every person in the workforce today should master the skill of scanning the horizon.

☙ **WHAT TO DO**: The point of this Experience is to help you scan for needs you could help address in your team, department or organization.

There are two parts to this Experience. First, we'll scan the biggest picture possible by focusing on trends that are impacting your industry or organization. Then, we'll zoom in to the smaller picture to assess how your department or team is doing.

Why would I do that?

This is important legwork to help you create the work opportunities in your current situation where you can deploy your professional passions (your VIEW) while helping the organization achieve its VIEW.

TIP › IF YOU ARE SELF-EMPLOYED

or between jobs, not all questions will apply, but you can still benefit from the experience.

If you are self-employed, consider:

> What trends are impacting your own company?

> What trends are impacting your clients or their industries?

If you are between jobs:

> What trends are impacting the industries or companies you are considering or applying to?

Here is a list of general trends that impact every organization, field or industry. How are these trends impacting your organization's mission, vision and goals? Circle the ones that apply or add your own. Write your notes and observations in the space provided.

Trend	Is/will your organization be impacted by:	How will your organization be impacted? Your Job?
Technology	‣ *Virtual reality* ‣ *Genetic engineering* ‣ *Automated vehicles* ‣ *Robots* ‣ *Embedded technologies* ‣ *Something else*	
Demographics	‣ *More Millennials* ‣ *Fewer Baby Boomers* ‣ *Multiculturalism* ‣ *Diverse perspectives and ways of thinking* ‣ *Family-leave policies* ‣ *Something else*	
Geopolitics	‣ *Rise of new markets* ‣ *Expansion in different countries* ‣ *Stability or instability in different regions* ‣ *Something else*	
Other?	*What other big-picture trends and changes might impact your organization, for example government regulations, global climate change, industry expansion or consolidation?* ‣ *Something else?*	
What would you say is the most relevant change impacting the organization?		

Let's zoom in a little closer, to scan for opportunities to help your department or team perform its best. What's working well? What could help your manager or team improve performance?

I'm not sure where this is heading.
You are learning how to be even more proactive in creating work experiences that enable you to live your VIEW *and* help your boss, team and organization. You are learning how to identify work possibilities for yourself that solve a problem or create opportunity for the organization, your department or team that's a win-win

TIP >IF YOU ARE SELF-EMPLOYED

If you are self-employed: You can apply the questions to your own team or to a customer or client.

If you are between jobs: This part of the Experience won't be as relevant to you now. Still, you can:

> Think about a team you recently worked with; see what insight you gain from the experience.

> Do this Experience when you've landed in your new workplace, so you can apply the skill of scanning the environment to your new situation.

WHAT TO DO: Think about your boss, department or team. How are things going? If you manage or lead a team, you could consider your team of reports, or the leadership team of which you are a part. You may also do the exercise both ways. Refer to the worksheet on the next page.

1. Check the box that best represents how your manager, team and/or department are performing against the qualities provided.

2. In the worksheet write notes for how you could help improve. You don't have to complete every box. Focus on the things that seem most practical to you right now.

Your Manager/Team Assessment

In my team or department. . .	None of the time	Some-times	All of the time	Ways I could help the team improve this are
My manager creates a clear set of goals for me that map to the organization's goals.				
My manager delegates to me effectively.				
Everyone on my team is clear about their roles and responsibilities. Everyone knows the "owner" for a task or project.				
Everyone knows how decisions will be made.				
Team members are cross-trained so we can back one another up.				
The team operates by a clear set of norms or agreements for how people will work for one another. Everyone lives up to these norms.				
The team works effectively with other teams or departments that are crucial to the success of the team or department.				
The team communicates effectively with one another. People are rarely blindsided with new information.				

Step back and review the list. If you work in an organization, is there one problem or opportunity you can help your manager, team, department or organization address? Here is a list of examples:

- Help the team repair an important relationship with another department.

- Lead a team meeting to clarify roles, decision making or operating procedures.

- Be more proactive in your day-to-day communications with people so you help everyone geton the same page.

- Offer to teach a teammate a new skill, meet someone in another department, run a lunch-and-learn to inspire continuous learning.

- If you are self-employed, what opportunities do you notice in your client's situations? Use thepower you have to improve situations for everyone.

1. Your Organization's View

Now, just like we did for your VIEW, write your organization's or Team's VIEW here:

_____

_____

_____

_____

_____

_____

Let's recap where we are with this week's Experiences. So far, you have:

Your VIEW:

- Reflected on when you find flow.

- Wrote an aspirational goal for your work for the next six months to one year.

The Organization's view:

- Scanned the Organization's goal and the trends that my help or get in the way of success.

- Scanned the team to identify opportunities for you to contribute to the teams' success.

Right now, the connection or Nexus between your VIEW and the organization's VIEW may not be obvious. This next Experience brings it all together.

ENGAGEMENT EXPERIENCE #9: YOUR NEXTIVITY
Time: 15–30 mins.

A development activity in the NeXus is a NeXtivity.

In the NeXus between your VIEW and the organization's VIEW are professional development activities that give you a chance to grow and challenge yourself while helping your boss, team or organization solve an important problem or capitalize on a new opportunity. A development activity in the NeXus is a *NeXtivity.*

You'll find an example of a NeXtivity on the next page, followed by a long list of ideas for activities to choose from or use for inspiration to create your own. You'll pull it all together with an easy-to-use blueprint for collecting and organizing your ideas. This will help you in Week 5, when you'll learn how to present a well-honed pitch and recruit your manager as an ally in creating your VIEW.

✏ **WHAT TO DO: Here's a blueprint for identifying your NeXtivity is on the next page. The three steps below prepare you to write your Action Plan:**

1. Review your work in Experience #7, "YOUR VIEW: An Aspirational goal" on page 91.

2. Review your work in Experience #8, "YOUR ORGANIZATION'S VIEW" on page 97.

3. Review the curated list of development activities that begins on on page 102. Find up to three activities that you believe fall in the NeXus between your VIEWand the needs of your team, department or organization. Circle or write them in the space below.

_____

_____

_____

_____

4. Use the template on the next page to write your Action Plan.

> **TIP > IF YOU ARE SELF-EMPLOYED**
>
> this template helps you think about projects or tasks you might propose to clients, to your mutual benefit.
>
> If you are between jobs, this template helps you get clearer about what you're looking for in a job, and perhaps identify specific tasks or projects you might volunteer to offer as a way of getting your foot in the door.

Week 3: Engagement: Your Action|Development Plan

Introduction: Now we'll put it all together, so you have a plan to increase your engagement and on-the-job development whether you work in an organization, for yourself, or you aspire to creating a new work opportunity.

✎ **WHAT TO DO: Use the template below to write your plan.**

1. Write your aspirational work goal:

_____

_____

_____

2. Write about needs you identified in your team, department or organization that you may be able to help address:

_____

_____

_____

3. Write about the possible NeXtivities. Refer to the long, curated list that begins on page 102 for ideas.

_____

_____

_____

	NeXtivity 1	NeXtivity 2	NeXtivity 3
Describe the NeXtivity			
How it helps me achieve my aspirational goal			
How it contributes to the team, department or organization			
Someone who can help			
How We'll Measure Success			

Example: Action | Development Plan

> 1. Write your aspirational work goal:

I would like to develop emotional intelligence, especially when it comes to negotiating more effectively with people. I feel like this is holding me back from being able to expand in my role.

> 2. Write about needs you identified in your team, *department or organization that you may be able to help address:*

Our team has a difficult relationship with the department next to us; we need to be able to work more effectively with them. We're not very skilled at negotiating deadlines, which causes frequent delays in delivering products.

> 3. Write about the possible NeXtivities. *In this example, the person chose three ideas from the curated list that begins on page 102.*

	NeXtivity 1	NeXtivity 2	NeXtivity 3
Describe the NeXtivity	*Read a book on emotional intelligence (also known as EQ).*	*Help build better relationships between your department or team and another department or team. Identify barriers to collaborating effectively and work to diminish or remove the barriers.*	*Find a colleague who has a skill you admire and would like to learn from. Ask the person if they would be willing to mentor you, share information or offer advice.*
How it helps me achieve my aspirational goal	*I n Week 2, I learned that I could be even more effective if I socialized my ideas with other people before plowing ahead and implementing them.*	*This could be an opportunity to build my EQ skills.*	*My colleague Alice knows how to get things done on the team. I think I could learn something from her.*

How it contributes to the team, department or organization	*I've caused some waves on the team by not taking other people's input into account.*	*It would be easier to get our jobs done if we could figure out how to work with the other team.*	*I think that some of my ideas would help the team work more efficiently, but I haven't done a very good job of getting people's buy in. If I succeed, our team could be even more productive.*
Someone who can help	*Alice is my peer and I feel comfortable checking in with her from time to time on how well I'm getting people's input.*	*Larry in Accounting has a good relationship with some of the people on that team. Maybe he could give me some insights into more effective ways of working with them.*	*Alice! I think I could ask her for advice and feedback more frequently.*
How We'll Measure Success	*I will take input from other people into account. Implementation will go more smoothly. Outcomes will be more effective.*	*We are sharing more information more often and that helps both teams improve their performance.*	*I really believe that some of my ideas could help the team. It would be great to see them implemented, and to see the relationships with some of my colleagues improve.*

Ideas and Examples of NeXtivities

Here is a curated list of ideas for NeXtivities:

Development NeXtivities for Work Enjoyment Goals:

☐ Review the results of your Best-Self Experience. How could you bring more of your Best Self to your work every day?

☐ Review the results of your Signature Skills Experience. What projects or tasks could you propose that would enable you to use more of your Signature Skills?

☐ Use your Signature Skills to shore up a skill or quality that you'd like to develop.

☐ Keep a gratitude journal of the things you enjoyed at work each day for one month. These things do not have to be earth-shattering. Perhaps you enjoyed lunch with a co-worker, or had a chance to put your Best Self or Signature Skills to work. You may be surprised by how much you actually enjoy in your current job.

Development NeXtivities for Behavioral Goals:

☐ Build your emotional intelligence muscles: Take a class or read about emotional intelligence. Some sources include,

> The Greater Good Science Center at University of California, Berkeley, which studies the psychology, sociology and neuroscience of well-being and teaches skills that foster happiness, compassion and resilience. http://greatergood.berkeley.edu

> Read a book or do some research on the topic of emotional intelligence.

> Take a deeper dive into INSIGHT by investing your time in one of these online self-assessments.

> The online Career Anchors Self-Assessment, which identifies your core career values. (There is a fee for this inventory.) https://www.careeranchorsonline.com/SCA/about.do?open=prod

> The Myers Briggs Type Indicator instrument, which helps you understand your energy source, preferred way of communicating, decision-making style and approach to lifestyle. (There is a fee for this inventory.) http://www.myersbriggs.org/my-mbti-personality-type/take-the-mbti-instrument/

☐ Identify a colleague with whom you have a challenging relationship. Learn more about emotional intelligence and work on ways to improve that relationship. See resources listed above.

☐ Nurture your creativity. Commit time on your calendar to visit or participate in a cultural event, such as an art museum or concert. Consider doing this alone so you can observe and reflect quietly.

☐ Be a mentor to a colleague. Offer your consistent, supportive ear. Learn how to coach effectively.

☐ Be mentored by a colleague. Accept another person's consistent, supportive ear. Learn how to be coached effectively.

☐ Help your manager find ways to communicate more effectively with the team, department and other stakeholders.

☐ Find a colleague who has a skill you admire and whom would like to learn from. Ask the person if they would be willing to mentor you, share information or offer advice.

Development NeXtivities for Expansion Goals:

☐ Build the connection between your organization and the community:

> Suggest an activity for your organization's volunteer corps.

> Participate in an activity in your organization's volunteer corps.

> Mentor or tutor a student.

☐ Become a problem solver:

> Propose a new process or system.

> Implement a new process or system.

> Take initiative to integrate processes or systems across teams or departments.

> Propose a new system, product, program or equipment for your team, department or organization.

> Participate in the sale of a product, system or program.

> Take charge of negotiating with a customer or with another team.

☐ Become a bridge builder:

> Troubleshoot problems on behalf of a dissatisfied customer.

> Run a task force on a business or community problem.

> Help build better relationships between your department or team and another department or team. Identify barriers to collaborating effectively and work to diminish or remove the barriers.

☐ Broaden your global experience and cross-cultural skills:

> Learn a new language.

> Learn about cross-cultural differences. (Check out www.Hofstede.com.)

> Visit a foreign country where your organization does business, even if the organization will not financially reimburse you.

☐ To deepen or expand your manager/leader experience, seek opportunities to manage different kinds of groups, including those that do not have to report to you, such as:

> People with less experience than you.

> People with more experience than you.

> People who used to be your peers.

> A cross-functional group dealing with a fix-it situation.

> A task force that is accountable for expanding or implementing a new market, office, product or service.

☐ Talk with your manager about how you would like to take on more responsibilities:

> Observe the tasks your manager currently owns but that could be delegated. Identify a task you could take on. Make it a win-win by identifying tasks that might boost your manager's success.

> Use the tips from "Recruit Your Boss" in Week 5 to have a NeXtivity discussion.

> Do a great job executing what has been delegated.

> Write a white paper about an opportunity and present it to top management.

☐ Gain management experience:

> Supervise an intern.

> Supervise a peer.

> Lead a cross-functional, virtual team.

☐ Represent and champion your team, department, division or organization in your industry:

> Support a corporate initiative. Help translate the corporate initiative into meaningful discussions and activities for your team, department or division.

> Help plan, lead or facilitate an offsite meeting or conference.

> Recruit on campus for your team, department, division or organization.

> Help with a key customer negotiation.

> Write a speech for someone higher in the organization.

> Present at a professional conference; represent the organization at panels, roundtables, etc.

☐ Become a champion for customers, internal and/or external:

> Identify a key customer-service improvement opportunity.

> Visit a customer site.

> Write a white paper about the customer experience with your product, organization, department or team. Present it to someone who is senior to you.

> Volunteer to serve on new project/product review committee.

☐ Create a thought-leadership platform in the NeXus. Thought leadership is your consistent sharing of new ideas and perspectives. You become a "thought leader" when people seek your insights and guidance in a particular topic area. A "platform" is a communication tool for elevating and communicating your ideas. A thought-leadership platform is comprised of the messaging and communication tools you use to get your ideas and perspectives out there.

☐ Refer to your VISION of your Best Self. What do you want to be known for? In what areas could you contribute new ideas and perspectives?

☐ Identify communication tools and approaches:

> Start a group that meets on a regular basis around a topic you care about. For example: innovation, change, communication or leadership.

> Start a blog.

> Contribute to the organization's portal or newsletter.

> Send news articles and links to information that will help your colleagues, reports manager and peers be more successful in their jobs.

> Write an Opinion-Editorial (Op-Ed) for a local newspaper on a topic you care about.

Development NeXtivities for Skill Goals:

☐ Become a more effective risk manager:

> Identify gaps in existing business-resumption plans.

> Identify threats to the reputation of the organization, product, department or team and offer solutions to address them.

> Learn about the different kinds of risk, both strategic and operational.

> Identify a problem and propose methods to address it.

☐ Strengthen your financial acumen and skills. Read the organization's annual report; or find free, online resources to strengthen your skill.

☐ Assign a challenging, complex project to one of your direct reports.

☐ Propose or design new approaches to measure individual or team effectiveness.

☐ Learn about a new trend or technique; summarize and present to others.

☐ Do a competitive analysis of how a team, department or organization offers a product or solves an important problem to learn best practices and apply them to your own team.

☐ Lead an "After-Action Review," or lessons-learned analysis with yourself, your team or department for:

> A successful project

> A failed project

> A meeting that went well

> A meeting that did not go as expected

☐ Become a product innovator:

> Scan the marketplace for trends and identify market or product opportunities. Write a white paper and propose it to someone senior to you.

☐ Learn more about change management:

> Study change management of other teams/customers/competitors.

> Present your findings and insights at a team, division or organization meeting.

> Identify ways in which you can support change efforts.

> Create a symbol for change.

> Be a change-champion for existing change efforts.

> Plan or facilitate an offsite meeting, conference, convention.

☐ Network with other thought leaders and people who share your values and interests.

> Become active in a member-organization.

> Volunteer on committees and task forces.

> Be willing to fund your membership even if your organization does not.

☐ Identify a process-improvement opportunity in your team or department.

> Write a white paper describing an opportunity.

> Offer to lead a process-improvement effort.

☐ Learn more about innovation:

> Identify incremental innovations that could help the team, department or organization.

> Study innovation of customers/competitors.

> Present your findings and insights at a team, division or organization meeting.

☐ Build your skills for working in a globally connected world.

> Learn another language.

> Visit an organization site or attend a conference.

Development NeXtivities for Movement Goals:

☐ Learn more about criteria for promotion inside your organization. Most companies want to see people performing at the next level before awarding a promotion. Do an honest self-assessment about whether or not people already see you performing at the next level. Refer to Week 2: Insights. Write your reasons why you are already performing at the next level and have earned a promotion.

☐ Interview someone in the organization who has a job that you aspire to. Learn about his or her career path. Colleagues are often open to helping other people in the organization.

☐ Job-shadow a colleague or work peer for short periods in other departments.

☐ Interview someone who has started his or her own business in your area of interest. Identify resources in your area, such as Small Business Association or other specialty groups that can offer insight and support as you consider taking a step toward self-employment.

Development NeXtivities for Performance Goals:

☐ Do an analysis of how you are spending your time. Write a plan to reallocate how you currently spend your time and energy so you are more productive and engaged.

Development NeXtivities Outside of Your Organization:

☐ Serve on a nonprofit board.

☐ Identify an intermediary in the school system of your city or town. Intermediaries are groups that help connect youth with work opportunities. If your organization does not already have a relationship with an intermediary, help create one. If your organization does have an intermediary, hire a youth as a summer intern. You'll gain valuable supervisory experience while helping a young person build employment skills.

☐ Volunteer to improve some aspect of the town or city in which you live or work. For example, help organize a civic improvement event, a charity run, or a food bank drive.

ENGAGEMENT WRAP-UP AND REFLECTION

ENGAGEMENT enables you to use your Signature Skills and be your Best Self every day so you feel greater fulfillment and flow. The goal of this week's exercises was to help you chart the development activities that expand the NeXus between your VIEW and the organization's goals.

This week, you . . .

- **wrote an aspirational goal** for your work life for the next six months to one year.

- **scanned the horizon,** to step back and take a more strategic look at your organization's business needs and the ways you might help your department or team operate more effectively.

- **identified three NeXtivities.**

Practice Box >

Commit to One Daily ENGAGEMENT Practice

A practice is an action you do every day with the intention to improve. For the next week, do at least one of these practices each day, to achieve greater ENGAGEMENT. You don't have to do them all—just choose the ones that work best for you and your situation. For each of these practices, refer to the list of suggested NeXtivities for specific ideas and suggestions.

➤ *Do one thing each day to improve your experience of flow.*

➤ *Scan the horizon for trends that are impacting the industry, company or job you are in.*

➤ *Use a Signature Skill with intention to compensate for an area of weakness.*

Next Week: WILL

WILL

is your capacity to choose your mindset, feelings and

actions with intention. It isn't enough to dream and reflect

on your VISION and INSIGHT, or to take a few steps toward

ENGAGEMENT. The strength of your inner resources of

WILL, including mind-body connection, makes them

happen. This doesn't mean you're alone. On the contrary.

When you lean on your Mentoring Network, you find

strength from the circles of people you bring together for

mutual exchange of ideas, feedback, practical resources,

new connections and support. You help one another

build WILL.

WILL

FEATURED EXPERIENCES:

🔟 Name Your Mountain

⓫ Your Mentoring Network

⓬ Your Mind-Body Nexus

Wrap-Up, Reflection and Practice

LET'S TALK ABOUT YOUR SUPERPOWER: WILL.

WILL is your capacity to choose your mindset, thoughts, feelings and actions with intention. I want to say this again because it is such a potent idea. WILL is the personal, deep, inner resource you draw upon when you want to take charge of how you think, feel and do when you make choices to take charge of your VIEW. Sometimes, as my friend Eileen, a respected former human resources executive, likes to say, "You do what you have to do in order to create what you want."

OK, so we're talking about willpower, right?

No.

Willpower is just one of the inner resources of WILL. Willpower is "the ability to resist short-term temptation to meet long-term goals," says the American Psychological Association (APA).[33] You grit your teeth and muscle through a task or situation. Willpower is self-discipline; the ability to delay gratification, override negative thoughts and self-regulate, essential qualities for personal well-being and development. Have you ever felt guilty over your lack of willpower? Participants in an APA survey ranked lack of willpower as "the number one reason for not following through" with changes they aspired to in their lives, such as exercising regularly, eating for health or saving for retirement.[34] Like a weight-lifter's bicep, you can strengthen your willpower.

The problem: Some experts say if you try to accomplish too many challenging goals at once, your willpower gets depleted.[35]

WILL, on the other hand, is abundant. *The power of WILL cannot be depleted.* When inner reserves run low and there's no more energy or willpower to tap, WILL offers a cornucopia of both internal and external resources that you can reach for. Your capacity to bring VISION, INSIGHT and ENGAGEMENT to life is equal to your capacity of WILL.

We are lucky to live in a time when researchers have greater understanding of the positive, inner resources that strengthen your WILL. Every day, new research emerges on topics like emotional intelligence, positive psychology, mind-body connection, and how your social circle influences how you learn. Through practice, you can build your inner resources. Here are just a few examples:

- **Mindfulness**, the moment-to-moment self-awareness of our thoughts and feelings, boosts our well-being and may help build leaders' self-confidence, according to researchers at University of California Berkeley.[36]

- **Resilience** can help you change corporate culture, even when you don't have formal power, say researchers Karen Reivich and Andrew Shatte.[37]

- **Growth** mindset leads to greater achievement because we "worry less about looking smart and put more energy into learning," says author Carol Dweck.[38]

- **Gratitude** lifts your mood and motivates you to be helpful to others.[39]

- **Empathy** can be used to more deeply understand ideas, art and people, says author Karla McLaren.

- **Compassion** makes better leaders, inspires teams and improves the customer experience, says Google engineer, TED-Talk speaker and One Billion Acts of Peace founder Chade-Meng Tan.

- **Grit** is one of the best predictors of elite performance from the classroom to the workplace, says renowned psychologist Angela Duckworth.

- **Happiness.** People who are happy experience more success in nearly every domain of life, including "work, health, friendship, sociability, creativity and energy," researcher and happiness advocate Shawn Anchor discovered.[40]

- **Ease,** says conscious embodiment guru Wendy Palmer, is the result of shifting our body patterns so brain chemistry shifts the mind.[41]

- **Presence,** says TED-Talk guru Amy Cuddy, is the physical manifestation of mindfulness and your Best Self, which can boost your confidence and effectiveness.

Whew!

I confess that creating the Experiences for this week required me to exert some willpower when it came to choosing what to include, because I would love to share everything.

Rather than inundate you with every finding, tip or tool, I've curated what I believe are the high-level resources most easily available as you take charge of your WILL. You'll gain self-awareness of what helps or holds you back from fulfilling your VIEW through the lens of your intentional—and unintentional—choices. You'll become more self-aware of the mind-body connections that strengthen or weaken your WILL, and you'll begin to create the supportive network you need to help you make the best choices toward the life and career of your dreams.

Think·Feel·Do This week, you will:

Name your Mountain. *What is something challenging that you want to do but find impossible to believe you could accomplish? This Experience will encourage you to name the challenge and* **to think** *about intentional and unintentional choices you are making.*

Identify one mind-body practice *that will boost your inner resources. Research on the mind-body connection continues to blossom and it's lucky for us: Breath, posture and your body are resources for WILL! These Experiences will enable you* **to feel** *more in tune with your body and how it helps or hinders your ability to choose your mindset, emotion or action in the moment..*

Build your Mentoring Network. *No one can go the journey alone. Research shows that when you create a supportive network of people you are more likely to find satisfaction, achieve your dreams and overcome challenges. This experience will enable you* **to do**

Outcomes for this week:

- Your acknowledgment of the real barrier(s) holding you back.

- Your Mentoring Network.

- One new mind-body practice that will help you be more intentional in how you choose to think, feel or act.

Why?

- "Everything pulls on everything." If you are struggling with or avoiding a challenge in one part of your life, it may be impacting another.

- Change happens. Tomorrow, the organization you work for could be bought, a competitor could enter the market and the product or program you work on could become obsolete in an instant. Opportunity, challenge and crisis will come into your life. WILL helps you thrive.

- By training your body and brain to strengthen your skill for choosing with intention, you are expanding your professional capabilities. This skill is essential for VIEW; for living your best life.

WILL EXPERIENCE #10: NAME YOUR MOUNTAIN
Time: 5–15 mins.

Deep in the heart of the White Mountains of New Hampshire, Mount Washington lords over the valley and challenges cyclists with the steepest bicycle race course in the continental United States. The road twists and turns upward for 7.3 miles at an average grade of 15 percent. To reach the finish line, cyclists grind up a 22 percent slope for the last 200 yards. It's so daunting that even car drivers have bumper stickers boasting *This Car Climbed Mount Washington*. My youngest brother, Joe, pedaled to victory twice, once in college and then again after graduate school.

Joe wrestled in high school and cycled the hills of our hometown without breaking a sweat. I played guitar, sang with the choir and starred in the high school production of *Oklahoma*. Where Joe was lean and strong like a mountain lion, I was chubby and soft like an overfed puppy. Inspired by my brother, I secretly desired to conquer that mountain too. *Someday*, I thought, *I'll start training for the race*. But I pictured my thick thighs in those skinny, black shorts and kept putting it off. What if I finished dead-last? What if the other cyclists laughed?

When I turned 30, I chose to stop being afraid and started sprinting hills in my neighborhood and commuting to work by bike. Feeling anxious but prepared, I registered for the race. On the morning of the race, I awoke in our hotel room in Conway, New Hampshire, with a pounding heart. But when we showed up at the start line, race officials said the climb was cancelled due to bad weather at the mountaintop. The following year, in my second attempt, the gun went off but as I rode past the tree line, the temperature plunged to 38 degrees Fahrenheit. Around mile six, the driving rain and bitter wind slapped my legs until they froze like ice sculptures and I could not push the pedals. The bike tipped toward the road's edge and went down into the gravel. I crossed the finish line, my head bowed with embarrassment, in a "sweep truck."

It took every bit of grit I could summon to try a third time. But now, I knew better. I prepared more effectively. During the race, I took short breaks. As my bike climbed, the valley unfolded below; the air became light and crisp. My spirits soared as I pedaled confidently past mile six, where I had fallen in my second attempt. When I crossed the finish line, Joe gave me a little boost up the final 50 feet. (Hey, don't judge—you should see that thing, it's nearly vertical!)

The mountain I needed to conquer, it turned out, was not the bike race itself. It was the invisible climb from my comfort zone of self-doubt to the discomfort of showing up at the start line. The experience wasn't pleasant. But by accepting unpleasant feelings as part of the process, I learned to be comfortable with challenge. I scaled the walls of my fear and transformed the discomfort into a source of inner strength and resolve.

I learned that everyone has his or her own mountain to climb. As the story circulated, friends told me about their dreams and how they chose to face down their fears and pursue them. One friend, Kim, overcame her self-doubts about being able to participate in any kind of athletic event and went on to become a regular at Boston's Tufts 10K road race for a few years. Another friend, Marge, took on a large fundraising project she didn't believe she was qualified to lead and shattered the previous records.

As a coach, I see leaders in the workplace who face their own mountains. Michelle, the nonprofit executive from the Introduction, needed to let go of the mindset that she had to do everything herself. She needed to delegate and develop others, her stakeholders said. In spite of this INSIGHT, she chose to stay stuck in her comfort zone, doing things herself instead of managing the work of others. "You have an action plan. What's holding you back?" I asked. It was scary to let go and trust the team, she said. What if she couldn't be successful? What if they all failed because she delegated? How could she cope with the loss of her identity as the go-to person, the one with all the answers, and develop her team to become that instead? The climb was too daunting for Michelle.

Michelle was choosing fear over WILL. So we had an honest conversation about whether she was actually passionate about being a manager. Would an individual-contributor path suit her VIEW more realistically? For a few meetings, she soul-searched. She truly loved her job; mentoring and developing others was part of her VISION. She determined she wanted to become the best manager she could. This time, instead of making plans for how Michelle could take action, we tried a different approach. What happened next may raise your eyebrow in doubt because it sounds a little crazy.

Michelle created one practice—an action she did every day with the intention to improve—that involved a bracelet she always wore. Michelle used the bracelet to be self-aware of her fear in the moment so she could choose to delegate with intention. In her office, whenever a problem came to her attention and poked at her impulse to do the task herself, she switched the bracelet to the opposite wrist *before acting*. This subtle maneuver gave her a moment to pause and step back to consider who else might perform the task and how she could support their success. That was the breakthrough she needed: not an action plan but a practice for strengthening her WILL. Progress followed. This wasn't a magic-wand moment that waved away her impulses. Today, she doesn't always choose the best response in the moment. But the bracelet reminds her of her commitment to tackle her mountain and strengthen her WILL.

If you are a people manager/leader, perhaps you've noticed a pattern in the stories about other manager/leaders with respect to delegating effectively. Delegating is about learning to let go, to embrace a new mindset about what defines you and your success. Your old version of your Best Self—the roles, tasks or projects you insist on holding on to—are holding you back. While the reasons are varied and personal to each individual, the bottom-line lesson is always the same. From the C-Suite to frontline supervisors, we need to let go in order to grow and reach the potential of the next Best Self version of ourselves. Only then can you bring out the Best Self of others.

Here are other examples of the mindset, emotions and thoughts we may choose to guide our actions. Maybe these resonate with the mountain you struggle to climb:

It has to be perfect. If it isn't perfect, people will laugh or I won't be able to meet my own high standards.

They'll find out I'm not as good as they think I am.

So and so is better than me.

I have to prove that I can do it all. Only weak people get help.

The other shoe's going to drop.

"Everything pulls on everything," the physical therapist told my son Ben. What's true for the body is true for our WILL. Maybe there is a mountain you would like to climb. It doesn't have to be related to work; it's all connected.

⅏ **WHAT TO DO:** Think about your answers to these questions. Then, write a letter to yourself.

➤ *What's your mountain? What inner challenge prevents you from showing up at the start line? Here are some tips to help you discover your answer. You don't have to write down the answers to all of these questions. They are just food for thought.*

» *What's something you've always wanted to have or to try in your life or work? Look back at your VISION for clues. What's been easy to pursue? What's been hard? Where are you in the journey?*

» *Look back at your reflections on INSIGHT. What Signature Skills do you most enjoy using? What do you want to learn or do but feel afraid or intimidated to try?*

» *Look back at your reflections on ENGAGEMENT. What's easy to try? What do you want to try, but are avoiding because it might be hard?*

» *What thread runs through your reflections on VISION, INSIGHT, and ENGAGEMENT?*

➤ *What is your mountain about?*

» *What thoughts run through your mind as you think about this mountain?*

» *How do you feel?*

» *What would it mean to you to show up at the starting line?*

➤ *What choices do you have for acting?*

» *What's the worst thing that will happen if you choose to scale your mountain? Can you live with that?*

» *What will happen if you choose to do nothing?*

➤ *Who can help?*

» *What support do you need?*

» *Who in your circle of friends, family and colleagues can help?*

Write a letter to yourself here.

WILL EXPERIENCE #11: YOUR MENTORING NETWORK
Time: 25-35 mins.

No one climbs their mountain alone.

For my third attempt up Mount Washington, I asked for help. My father, who had cycled thousands of miles from the time he was 14, coached me on training rides. My husband pitched in with childcare so I could commute to work by bicycle and work up a sweat. The night before the race, my mother cooked a pasta dinner then waited at the top of the mountain for hours while we raced up so she could drive us all down. I could not have overcome the mountain without the help of my support team.

In my travels, I meet people at all levels who crave the help of a support team. Mostly, people tell me they want to find a mentor. Perhaps you also long to find a champion who can open doors, provide information, listen with empathy, share his or her experience and generally be in your corner when it comes to your career. Researchers have found that when you create a network of mentors who supply support, you can do all the things you hope for and more. I call this your Mentoring Network.

What is a Mentoring Network and how can it help me?

Forget the traditional image of a wise sage passing down advice or a boss whose coattails propel you to the top. Your Mentoring Network is a constellation of people who both coach and learn with you throughout your life and career. Each relationship is a win-win. You listen, advise, give feedback and comfort to one another along the journey toward your VIEW. Learning is social. You learn more about yourself through exchanges with others. Open yourself to the possibility that your best mentors are right in front of you from all the social and professional circles in your life: colleagues and classmates past and present, friends, family, people from book clubs, sporting or music clubs, religious groups and many others.

Your current colleagues can offer a special source of mentoring support: Professor Emeritus Kathy Kram at Boston University conducted groundbreaking research that shows even a small, active network inside your organization can lead to "loyalty, good performance and promotion within." Mentors can help you make career moves within your organization, but also move "from one organization to another, or one particular industry to another," Kram says.[42]

A vibrant Mentoring Network boosts your resilience. In one study of careers across the globe, Professor Tim Hall of Boston University and his colleagues found that people with INSIGHT who also activate their Mentoring Network in tough times bounced back more quickly from setbacks.[43] In contrast, people who did not have these supportive, individualized learning networks suffered more setbacks and took longer to bounce back. Your Mentoring Network is essential to your VIEW. "Your network is your net worth," a colleague likes to say.

How does a Mentoring Network contribute to the strength of my WILL?

WILL is your capacity for choosing your mindset, emotions and actions with intention. The people in your Mentoring Network can help you rise above, reflect on your experiences, and offer a fresh point of view on where you want to go and the choices you are making. Although your mentors can help with job networking and moves, you do so much more for one another. You help one another solve problems, get unstuck, face how you're feeling about a situation so you can figure out a plan to move beyond it. Together, you help one another build the inner and physical resources you need to take charge of your VIEW. With a Mentoring Network, you're never alone.

Can you give me a few examples of a Mentoring Network?

Absolutely. You could:

- **Convene a group of people** who can serve as your personal Board of Directors (BOD), a collection of your top-level advisors who each have different skills and experience and who can meet with you every four to six months. My personal BOD is very small (just five or six people) and consists of friends who don't always agree with how I see the world; family members who have influenced my life and career; and colleagues past and present who have earned my trust because they will be straight with me. Since my BOD members are far-flung across the United States, I can't meet with them at the same time and in person. So, instead, I set up conversations periodically and ask for their help reflecting on where my consulting business has been and where it is going next. And, most importantly, I return the favor.

- **Identify a thought leader in your field** or industry who shares your passion for your work and may be willing to spend some time helping you sort through your ideas and dreams. Tim Hall, Professor Emeritus at Boston University, has served this role for me for many years, including when he mentored me on the first academic paper I published, which was on the topic of career development. The cost of his time is usually a cup of coffee. Often, he has a question or two for me in return.

- **Ask one or two colleagues** who work closely with you, including your boss if you're comfortable, to give you candid feedforward periodically, especially when you know you are facing a difficult situation that triggers your "dinosaur brain," which we discussed in INSIGHT. My colleagues at Prior Consulting serve this role for me. It can be tough to ask the question, "How am I doing?" when you work so closely with people, but their honest answers help me be a better leader and person.

You and your Mentors decide how often you'll connect. For example, you and a colleague could meet regularly to coach each other; you could ask a senior leader to coffee a few times or call on a member in your community to meet once to offer perspective or advice.

What if I have more introverted energy or feel reluctant to reach out to ask for help? My advice: Take your time; build your Mentoring Network in small steps. Begin with one of your most powerful, personal resources: your inner world of deep reflection and thought. For example, you could start by writing a mentoring letter to yourself. On the top of a blank page, write your own Question & Answer about a challenge you are facing. Getting anchored in your thoughts will help you feel more comfortable as you reach out to others. Then, you could ask a trusted friend for advice and offer something in return. Quality, not quantity, matters.

OK, you're saying that it's useful to have variety in my Mentoring Network. Can you say more about how to make the relationships win-win?

Different people have something unique to offer; you have something unique to give.

Here are a few ideas of what you could exchange:

You could ask for . . .	You could offer . . .
feedforward.	to reciprocate on something you ask for.
a "sounding board" for a new idea.	anything on the list to the left.
help with a resume.	a helpful tip, article, book or idea.
help with making a new connection or contact.	to treat for coffee or lunch.
advice.	to volunteer for something.

๑ **WHAT TO DO:** This week, you'll draft your own plan for a Mentoring Network and begin to reach out to people. You will work at a pace that matches your energy and available time.

> *Begin by writing an intention for your Mentoring Network. The examples below offer ideas.*

Examples

I need to get out of my shell and meet people in my field. Within the next six weeks, I'd like to meet one new person and learn more about his or her job. Since I'm a little bit shy or reluctant in these kinds of situations, I will ask a trusted colleague to introduce me to the person. In exchange, I can help the person develop a technical skill or tell the person about the job or department where I work. That way, we can each learn more about the organization where we work and have a new contact to call on for information or advice.

Within the next six weeks, I will identify a few people who can serve as a "'Board of Directors" who can meet with me twice a year to review my progress toward my VIEW. Like the board of directors of an organization, they can offer guidance and feedback on my progress toward my VIEW and can help me hold myself accountable for achieving my goals. My board of directors will include people from different parts of my life —one family member, a friend, a colleague and one community member. I will share my VIEW with them and ask for their perspective on my progress. If I can't get them all together in the same room, I will meet with them one-on-one or in small groups. In exchange, I could offer to serve on each person's "board."

I would like to implement one of the Development Activities I identified during Week 3: ENGAGEMENT. I could use help from someone who has perspective and experience and can offer advice for how I could propose this activity to my manager. In exchange, I could offer this person something that I think could be useful to achieving their own goals, whether at work or in their careers.

Now, use the Action Plan template to help you create your Mentoring Network.

Now, turn your ideas into an action plan.

Here is an Example:

Who:	From My Circle of:	What I hope to gain:	What I can offer:	When: I will reach out to this person by...	Support: Someone who can help is . . .
Amy Richardson	*Colleagues*	*I know Amy only from a distance and I'd love to learn more about her work and career path.*	*Help her make a new connection in my department.*	*Friday, one week from now.*	*My manager knows Amy and might help me make a connection.*
John Smith	*Friends*	*Feedback on the Development Activities I want to propose to my manager or team.*	*Articles on some of the technical things I know he is interested in.*	*Friday, one week from now.*	*I am comfortable reaching out to John on my own.*

Your Turn:

	Who:	What I hope to gain:	What I can offer:	When: I will reach out to this person by...	Support: Someone who can help is . . .
1.	Colleague				
2.	Family				
3.	Friend				
4.	Social Group				
5.	Professional Group				

➤ *Right now, before you turn the page, draft an email or text to the three people on your list and schedule your first mentoring conversation. Here are examples of what you could say:*

　　» *I'm passionate about achieving a professional goal and pulling together a network of Mentors to turn to over the next year. It wouldn't be a big commitment of your time, and I would like to reciprocate by supporting something you're trying to achieve.*

　　» *Would love to get together to hear your perspective or advice on something I'm working on.*

　　» *I'm struggling with a challenging situation and wonder if you'd be willing to be a sounding board and help me think it through.*

　　» *I could use some mentoring about a possible opportunity. Your experience is amazing and I'd value your advice. Can I treat for coffee next Tuesday?*

WILL EXPERIENCE #12: YOUR MIND-BODY NEXUS
Time: 15–30 mins.

When you feel calm in your body, you experience ease in your mind. With ease, you can more fully be your Best Self, even in stressful moments. Your body is a great source of WILL if you learn to tune in and choose to be mindful.

Researchers at Greater Good Science Center, University of California at Berkeley, say that mindfulness is "maintaining a moment-by-moment awareness of our thoughts, feelings, bodily sensations and surrounding environment."[44] Being mindful of your thoughts and feelings requires you to also be mindful of your body's response. With this awareness, you can recruit your body to help you choose your response, to strengthen your WILL. There's a flood of information about mindfulness, presence and mind-body connection in books and online. My goal is to help you sort through some of the essentials, and to offer practical tools you can use to recruit your body to support your mind and WILL. In this short, curated list, I've chosen three:

- The Strange Hiding Places of Stress

- The Power of Sleep

- The Peculiarities of Power Poses

Why these three tools of mindfulness?

1. The research behind these three topics is reasonably robust.

2. The topics do not overlap. They can build upon and support one another.

3. Each topic offers at least one tool or approach you can experiment with immediately, even while you are reading. Well, maybe except the sleep topic. Before you nap, I encourage you to at least finish reading the chapter.

The Strange Hiding Places of Stress

Roberta Kraus was the tallest person in the room; she wore a handcrafted silver-and-turquoise necklace and a USA track suit. Before her, in an intimate setting, were 40 business executives, men and women from all over the United States, participating in a conference on neuroscience and leadership among the gently rolling hills of Colorado Springs. Self-assured, Roberta walked from one side of the small conference stage to the other with ease. A captivating figure with a hearty smile, she commanded our attention. We were willing participants because we knew that she was about to share the same secrets for top, consistent performance that she used in her coaching with CEOs and Olympians.[45]

A pioneer in the field of mind-body learning and a former Alternate to the Olympics herself, Roberta served as Senior Faculty and Sports Psychologist with the Center for Creative Leadership (CCL) for nearly 30 years. She introduced herself, told us about her experiences as part of the coaching staff at the U.S. Olympic Training Center in Colorado Springs and shared some highlights of the latest research. All of which you would expect, since that's why we had gathered together in the first place. Just at the point when we'd settled back comfortably listening to her lecture, Roberta hit us with something uncomfortable.

"Think of a conflict or conversation you recently experienced," Roberta said. "Imagine the person, the room or location you were in and the situation that caused you to feel stress."

The room grew quiet. A few participants grimaced.

"Really get into it," Roberta encouraged. "What was the source of the conflict? What emotions did you feel? Were you angry? Afraid? Did you want to fight? Run away?"

Some people shifted side-to-side in their seats. I confess I was among them.

"Now, hold that feeling, *feel* that feeling," Roberta said. "And tell me, where is your tongue?"

Eyes widened. *What an odd question.* And yet nearly everyone in the room had the same response.

"On the roof of my mouth," we said in unison. Roberta smiled, as if she knew we'd all have this answer.

"I call this 'tongue-technique,'" she said.

Cue the grown-up giggles.

"This is a great example of the mind-body connection," Roberta explained, smiling but ignoring the guffaws. "It's one way the body responds to stress and it's so subtle. I've been teaching the technique for many years. Group after group, person after person, this stress response has been universal. It's just one example of how, without our awareness or effort, the response to stress shows up in our bodies," she said.

If you followed along with Roberta's instructions above, imagining your own conflict or difficult conversation, did you find your tongue on the roof of your mouth? If you did, you may be wondering what's going on. Remember the amygdala, the tiny region of the brain with a big response to danger? When the amygdala senses conflict, it stimulates the release of cortisol, a stress hormone. Cortisol signals the body to protect itself from impending danger. Your body goes on high alert and prepares to defend itself from an attack. Everything tenses up. The tongue goes up to the roof of your mouth. For many, the jaw goes with it, followed by the neck and shoulders. If this happens to you, it could explain why your jaw or shoulders may ache at the end of the day; you've been on high guard, jaw clenched, shoulders scrunched. And just think, it all starts with your tongue pressing against the roof of your mouth.

In Roberta's "tongue-technique," simply noticing the position of your tongue in a stressful situation raises your awareness of how you're responding. Your tongue, like Michelle's bracelet from the WILL case study in the Introduction, is a resource for noticing your thoughts and feelings. With this self-awareness, you can choose your response. You can pull your tongue off the roof of your mouth, which tells the cortisol production to slow and your body to calm down. Your body wants to know that you are safe. You have to protect the body to help your mind feel secure. When you experience this calm, you are better able to choose your response or action in the moment. You are able to take charge of your WILL.

Reflection: Working with the head of distribution of a retail chain, I asked, "Where do you feel stress?" He immediately pointed to his legs. "In my calve muscles," he said. Other people have pointed to their lower backs or stomachs. Every person is different. Think about your answers to these questions

> *Where does stress show up in your body?*

> *How can you use this knowledge to help your body, and your mind, feel safe—so you can exercise WILL, choose your best response in the moment and not let your response be chosen for you?*

The Power of Sleep

When you were little, your parents probably made you go to bed, saying, "It's important to get a good night's sleep." But here's the thing your parents didn't realize: When you sleep, certain regions of your brain roll up their sleeves and go to work. This is what Dr. Jessica Payne, Associate Professor at Notre Dame University and a leading researcher on sleep, learning and memory, wants you to know.

Payne clicked her way through PowerPoint slides during a conference in Boston on neuroscience and leadership. She gestured with feeling and moved with the energy of someone who had gotten a good night's sleep. "The brain is intensely active during sleep, especially during the phase we call Rapid Eye Movement or REM. Regions of the brain that are important for learning, emotion, memory and cognition are more active while you are asleep than when you are wide awake," she told us. Think about that statement for a moment and what it means in relation to WILL, your capacity to choose thoughts and feelings and actions with intention. Most of the processing of the essential things that comprise your mindset, emotions and response happens without your conscious awareness.

This is such an important idea, it's worth saying in a different way: By getting high-quality sleep, you fortify WILL. Researchers like Payne say that with enough sleep, you can:

- Choose positive emotions, mindset and thoughts more easily

- Improve perspective, see pieces of the puzzle

- Remember stuff better

- Be more creative and productive

- Lift your mood, which means you are more likely to reach out to people for support or to offer help

Sleep deprivation weakens WILL by generating:

- A bias toward noticing and remembering negative over positive emotion

- Fragmented perspective

- Memory loss

- Fewer insights, loss of creativity

- Crankiness during your waking hours, which makes you less likeable. (Sorry, but it's true!) You'll be less willing to offer or receive support from others.

How much sleep is enough?

The standard advice, get eight hours of sleep each night, may not apply to you. How much sleep you actually need is a personal matter and connected to your own circadian rhythms, the 24-hour cycle of waking and sleeping, regulated by light and temperature. Payne says that on average people need eight hours of sleep, but for any individual person the number can be as low as five or as high as nine. Her research indicates that the number of hours may be important, but being consistent is even more important.

 And she's terribly excited about the potential of naps. "Naps are one of the most amazing insights to come out of the field of memory and sleep research in recent years. A daytime nap can in some cases get you at least as much bang for your buck as a full night's sleep, in terms of cognitive performance, and sometimes, it can get you even more." What makes a nap so powerful? "You're cleaning the cache, beginning to consolidate information so you can take in more information; the data aren't clear yet why, but there's compelling proof that naps work. And you don't want more than 20-minute naps, in fact ten or 15 minutes may be just fine. If you sleep too long, you risk going too deep and may wake up groggy."[46]

It's proven that lack of sleep impacts on-the-job performance. In a separate study, researchers found that 74 percent of participants in a survey said they "work while tired," while nearly 40 percent admitted that their sleep deprivation caused them to make mistakes. One sleep-deprived person confessed to accidentally issuing paychecks to everyone in the organization twice in the same week.[47]

Here is some practical advice from Dr. Jessica Payne about how to get the most from sleep:

- Power nap in ten-, 15- or 20-minute increments each day.

- If you can't get enough sleep, choose a "sleep proxy," including;

  » *a walk, especially in nature*

  » *exercise of your choice*

  » *ten-minute meditation*

  » *going offline for a little while*

- Alcohol may relax you in the moment, but it's shown to contribute to waking up at night. For your best night's sleep, choose to leave at least one hour between your favorite glass and going to bed, so it can metabolize.

- While you sleep, minimize distractions and light.

The bottom line: Sleep boosts your WILL; it's a crucial way to take care of yourself so you can take charge of your VIEW.

Power Pose

Would you believe that your posture is a resource for strengthening WILL?

The way you sit and stand can change the way you think and speak, says Wendy Palmer. A pioneer in the leadership field of "conscious embodiment," Palmer studied Aikido, a nonaggressive form of martial arts from Japan. "Falling and then quickly standing up in a new position without judgment is one of the gifts my body continues to receive from Aikido training. We call it 'the art of falling.' My whole being learned how to recover, adapt and go forward within situations that are continually unfolding," she said.[48] Palmer teaches about personal space; choosing a quality you wish to embody; and centering the body as a way to improve listening, inclusion, "big-picture thinking, creativity and intuition."

How your thoughts and feelings show up in the body is a practical matter, one that I see managers struggle with every day. Sue, a midlevel manager of an investment organization, had an "aha" moment as she watched her body language on a screen. She and a colleague had just completed a videotaped role play of a difficult conversation about his performance. Sue noted that her shoulders were hunched, and she leaned on the table as if it were holding her up. The quality Sue projected: anxiety. Before we rolled the camera a second time, she practiced centering her body for a few minutes—head up, chin level with the floor, shoulders balanced and at ease on her body.

Try this right now: Scrunch your shoulders up to your neck and hold them there to the count of five. Then, quickly drop your shoulders so they feel balanced on your body and level with the ground. Ah. That's how Sue felt. When we rolled the camera to give her a second shot at the role play, the quality of the exchange improved dramatically. She felt greater confidence and it showed. Her Best Self—the self-assured manager who had compassion for the person who needed to improve his performance—had shown up.

"Finding and believing in our authentic best selves can help us overcome threats that might otherwise undermine us during big challenges. But alone, it's still not enough to make us present during those challenges. After finding your authentic Best Self, you must figure out how to express it," writes Amy Cuddy, author of *Presence*,[49] and a TED-Talk speaker.

In case you are not one of the 35 million people who have seen her TED Talk, Cuddy recovered from a traumatic brain injury; surgeons said her IQ would drop and she would never have the same quality of thinking again. Through perseverance, Cuddy not only regained her intellectual abilities, but pursued groundbreaking research on the body and mind. She discovered that how you stand or sit affects both testosterone and cortisol levels in the brain.

Her breakthrough concept: power poses. Through the myriad studies Cuddy has reviewed and conducted, people who embodied their best selves put the body into poses that expanded personal space. They showed up with confidence, were more likely to earn investor funding for their projects, were more highly evaluated by a panel of job interviewers and, most importantly, felt good about themselves regardless of the outcome because they believed they had shown up with their Best Self.[50] Cuddy's main message: Power poses can rewire the mind.

Now let's connect the dots between Cuddy's research on power poses and your Best Self.

Do you remember the photo you took of your Diamond of Cards, as well as your written statement of your Best Self in Week 2: INSIGHT? Please go find them.

❧ **WHAT TO DO: Review your Best-Self reflections.** Have the qualities and traits you envisioned changed over the past few weeks? If your answer is yes, perhaps this means you've gained insight and self-awareness. If no, that's OK too. Perhaps your work over the past few weeks has reinforced the things you already knew about yourself.

With your Best Self in mind, imagine you are about to take on an action that requires courage, grit or resilience. Perhaps it's a presentation to a skeptical audience, a difficult conversation or asking someone you don't know very well for mentoring advice. How do you want to show up? What will success feel like for you after this action or event? To help you express this Best Self, here are just a few tips for mind-body awareness, including some of the poses Amy Cuddy's research suggests you might use to prepare:

DO:

- In the morning, or just before an event or difficult conversation, find a private space where you can expand into Cuddy's most famous power pose. Stand with your feet hip-width apart and hands on your hips for up to two minutes. Like a superhero.

- Be aware of the position of your shoulders. You'll feel more at ease when they are down, level and balanced.

- Mentally strike a power pose if you are in a situation where you can't do it physically.

DON'T

- Hunch over your mobile device, which robs you of assertiveness and increases the chance of neck pain and headaches.[51]

- Power pose when you're talking with someone. It can be intimidating and could actually detract from your intention.

- Scrunch your shoulders around your neck. This creates tension and signals weakness. In the wild, animals that hunt go for their victim's neck. Be the lion, not the lunch.

You have mind-body tools for strength training your WILL. Use mindfulness to help you locate stress hiding in strange places; feed your body the best-quality sleep for your needs; and adopt your own "power" practices to recruit your body in recharging and reshaping the mind. Take care of yourself as you take charge of your VIEW.

WILL Wrap-Up, Reflection and Practice

WILL is the capacity to choose our mindset, thoughts, emotions and actions with intention. WILL is abundant: There are so many resources both within and outside of ourselves that we can choose to cultivate.

We bring VISION, INSIGHT and ENGAGEMENT into our lives and work through the strength of our WILL.

Stopped in traffic on the I-90 just outside of Boston one day, I had time to notice the sticker on a car bumper. It read, "I am a human being and not a human doing." There's wisdom in this countercultural phrase. With so much change, complexity and ambiguity in the world, we find ourselves overscheduled, moving without a break from activity to activity, and not making time to renew ourselves physically, spiritually and emotionally. We need to pause from all the doing to refresh, rejuvenate and make space for the creativity and insight that are so essential to creating the things we desire in our lives and our work.

At the same time, I believe we can learn a lot about ourselves by doing, by putting ourselves into experiences that challenge and engage us, that have the potential for personal growth. Learning is a social process. We learn about ourselves through our relationships and exchanges with other people. The people we bring into our lives and work help strengthen our WILL, and we, in turn, support them. We are all co-learners with our own, unique VIEW on this planet.

Practice Box >

A practice is something you do every day with the intention to improve.[52] Look at the list of qualities and traits in the WILL introduction. For this week, use Wendy Palmer's practice: choose one quality from your Best Self you wish to embody this week. Begin your day with an intention for how you will practice this quality to strengthen your WILL.

Next Week: First, Recruit Your Boss. How can you recruit your boss and others to be allies in creating your VIEW? Next week, you'll learn how.

PART III:

Living Your VIEW

First, Recruit Your Boss

Do you have people who believe in you, including your

boss if you have one, to help you take charge of your

VIEW and chart your NeXtivity? Do you love your current

situation? Can you put your passions to work where you are

or do you find yourself on the fence overlooking greener

pastures? This week, you'll set the wheels in motion to

road-test your VIEW within your current situation. And if

you come up empty-handed after a few substantial efforts

to make things happen, I'll offer a roadmap for helping you

think through what to do next. By the end of this week,

you'll either be energized to recommit to where you are

now, or have considered the reasons for moving on to the

next leg in the journey of your life and career.

First, Recruit Your Boss

FEATURED EXPERIENCES:

13 **Prepare Your Pitch**

14 **Make Your Pitch**

15 **Commit or Go**

Wrap-Up, Reflection and Practice

THE WORK YOU DO TODAY COULD BE A GOLD **MINE** of opportunity for the future. Allies—people who are on your side and who believe in you, like your boss or a great client—are key to unlocking the hidden treasure. Whether you work for yourself or someone else, your business or job is one of the most crucial assets you've created. Journalist Barbara Kiviat of Time magazine wrote this after the financial crisis of 2008:

> *"In terms of the American psyche—and a household's balance sheet—we're rediscovering the job as the most valuable asset a person can have."*[53]

How do I recruit the support I need for my VIEW in my current situation?
Think back to our conversation about stakeholders in Week 2: INSIGHT. Stakeholders include not only the people who rely on your performance for their own work success or personal growth and satisfaction; they are also the people who can block the path to getting what you want. You start recruiting the support you need by embracing the possibility that when it comes to your work situation today, your boss may be your most important stakeholder relationship.

> **TIP >
> EVERYONE HAS A BOSS.**
>
> Even people who are self-employed are accountable to investors, clients, customers and possibly to your personal Board of Directors.
>
> If you are self-employed or between jobs, you'll find tips throughout the week to adapt the Experiences to your situation.

Everyone has a boss. Even people who are self-employed are accountable to investors, clients, customers, and possibly to your personal Board of Directors. Your boss has a huge stake in the success of your work; it is in your boss's best interests to support your NeXtivity. Are you in tune with your boss? How do you make the relationship a win-win? In your campaign to win the support of allies, your first step is to recruit your boss.

In one global study of careers, researchers from Boston University were surprised to find that people said that their boss was a helpful influence. The number was higher than the researchers expected. Maybe, like those study participants, your boss is great—a person who cares about you, gives feedback regularly and proactively helps you work toward what's next in your career.[54] Maybe your boss is terrible—a person who seems to care more about him or herself, keeps secrets, takes credit and hoards the best projects instead of delegating to you.

You now have your VIEW. Have you truly exhausted all options to mine in your current situation? Are there new gems of experience, skill and relationships for you to discover? Have you recruited your boss as an ally in the adventure?

Think·Feel·Do This week, you will:

Prepare Your Pitch. *Through six steps, you will draft your NeXtivity pitch to your boss. This Experience will encourage you to* **think**.

Commit or Go. *How do you feel about whether you want to stay or go? This Experience explores how you're* **feeling***. Do you want to stay where you are, or are you ready for greener pastures?*

Make Your Pitch. *Sometimes, the hardest step is knowing where to begin the conversation. This Experience will help. You'll learn how to compare your assumptions and expectations with your boss's or other allies so the conversation is more productive and maybe even more rewarding for you both. The Experience will encourage you to* **do**.

Outcomes for this week:

- A "pitch" for your NeXtivity, a development activity in the NeXus between your VIEW and the organization's.

- A roadmap for making your pitch.

- A roadmap to help you choose to find new energy and commitment in your current situation, or to move on in a win-win way.

Why?

- Your boss and other allies can help or hinder your VIEW.

- With limited resources in any workplace, your pitch will hone in on the win-win.

- You'll get more flow from your current situation if you feel fully committed; and if you feel you are ready to leave, there's a way to make your exit a win-win as well.

FIRST, RECRUIT YOUR BOSS EXPERIENCE #13: PREPARE YOUR PITCH
Time: 25–35 mins.

Your boss is like an investor with limited resources who must be allocated wisely. (If you're self-employed, your boss may actually BE your investor!) He or she needs to hear how your proposed NeXtivity will pay off for the team and the organization. Here is some guidance on how to draft your pitch.

A great pitch gets an investor excited about . . .

- the problem you're solving.

- what you're offering.

- the expected payoff.

How you pitch matters too! Entrepreneurs who showed up with confidence and were grounded in their image of Best Self ahead of the meeting had greater success than those who did not, according to a study by Amy Cuddy. Read through the examples below, then use the template to draft your pitch.

❧ **WHAT TO DO:** You've already done most of the work. Refer to your notes from the previous weeks as you use this template to write the four parts of your pitch.

Your PITCH	EXAMPLES
Here's my idea for a development activity. (Look back at your work in Week 3, ENGAGEMENT.)	**Example 1:** As a development goal, I'd like to strengthen my emotional intelligence in working with others. We have some opportunities to build better relationships with the QA team. I propose to spearhead a cross-department brown-bag lunch so we can learn about one another's work. **Example 2:** Our team has done some great work on XYZ and I think it would be both useful and inspiring to showcase this work inside and outside of the organization. As a career development goal, I'd like to work on my presentation skills. I propose to present our results at the upcoming trade conference.
How it is a win-win.	» Increases productivity, quality or performance. » Improves relationships with other departments, so work flows more smoothly and everyone enjoys their work more. » Improves my engagement and flow in my current role, so I am more productive and contributing at a higher level. » Gets the word out about the great things we're doing in our team/organization.
Resources I will need:	Time, financial support, team support, manager support, other
How will we measure success?	Improved quality, quantity, speed, efficiency, relationships; re-energized commitment and work satisfaction.

Your Pitch

Use this blank template to write your pitch.

Your PITCH	
Here's my idea for NeXtivity:	
How it is a win-win.	
Resources I will need:	
How will we measure success?	

_____

_____

_____

_____

_____

_____

_____

_____

_____

_____

_____

_____

_____

_____

_____

_____

_____

FIRST, RECRUIT YOUR BOSS EXPERIENCE #14: MAKE YOUR PITCH

Time: 2-3 hrs., including prep, conversation with your manager, and your post-meeting reflections.

How can you make your best pitch?

Prepare. Be grounded in your Best Self. Know your goals for the conversation. Be curious about your boss's perspective so you're sure to ask great questions and learn.

But above all, before you start pitching ideas, I encourage you to "level-set" your understanding of where you are in your current situation with respect to how you're doing. When you and your boss (or other allies) are level-set, you have a data-driven understanding of your current performance. I can't emphasize this point enough, so I'll say it in a slightly different way: Be certain that you and your boss have the same picture of your performance and that you're weighing the same things in terms of the outcomes you produce and what they mean. Are you using the same criteria or standards to evaluate success? Is what you accomplish more important than how you accomplish your goals? Do you have the same understanding of the challenges and barriers that lie between you and success? I find this is especially true when people pitch a promotion or significant expansion of responsibilities or projects to their boss.

Here's a sad example of what I mean:

Tony, a fundraiser, brought millions of dollars to the university where he worked and was sure he was ready for a promotion. His NeXtivity: to take on broader responsibility for managing people in the university's development office. When he pitched both the promotion and taking on more direct reports, the manager denied his request. Tony felt angry and disappointed. Besides bringing in major donors, he believed he'd demonstrated strong leadership skills. Tony blamed his manager for not seeing things his way but, from my perspective, Tony had caused his own disappointment due to self-deception. He hadn't made the effort to gather the appropriate data to look realistically at how his work effort was perceived.

The problem: Tony's manager told me he had participated in meetings where he saw Tony cut people off midsentence instead of listening, or gave orders when the situation called for asking for other people's input. Tony and his manager were not aligned in their understanding of both the criteria for promotion and Tony's performance. Ideally, Tony should have taken more initiative to get his manager's perspective *before* making his pitch. And his manager should have had more feedback discussions so that he and Tony understood each other's perspectives ahead of time.

Make sure you and your boss are operating within the same set of assumptions and perceptions before you talk about what's next in your career. Assumptions are hidden beliefs that we take so much for granted we're not even aware of them. Tony believed that raising funds was the most important criterion for promotion—an assumption he didn't even think to question. In contrast, Tony's manager believed that *how* Tony worked with others was just as important as achieving financial goals. Tony and his manager weren't just out of sync. They were using different scales.

Here are some tips:

- Begin by making sure you and your boss agree on how you're performing in your role today.

- Expect that this is not a one-shot event or conversation.

- Be flexible but persistent. Progress will unfold over several, well-prepared conversations.

- Prepare to do most of the talking. This conversation is about you and your VIEW. Each time you get up to bat, you want to be confident and prepared.

- Emphasize the win-win.

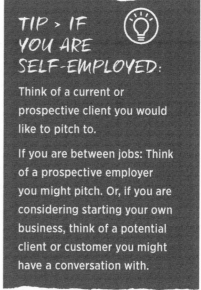

TIP > IF YOU ARE SELF-EMPLOYED:

Think of a current or prospective client you would like to pitch to.

If you are between jobs: Think of a prospective employer you might pitch. Or, if you are considering starting your own business, think of a potential client or customer you might have a conversation with.

Make Your Pitch: A Roadmap

✎ WHAT TO DO: Follow these six steps to jumpstart a NeXtivity pitch with your manager. Details follow on the next few pages.

Before You Pitch Your Boss

	WHAT TO DO	TIPS
Step 1	✎ Draft your NeXtivity pitch.	Use Experiences #7, #8, #9 for ideas. Experience #13 (the previous experience) includes an easy-to-follow template.
Step 2	Before you schedule the meeting with your boss or other ally, write your goals and define success for the conversation. Ask yourself two questions and write your answers. *What is my goal? Here are examples:* ➤ *I want to get feedback on how my boss thinks I'm doing in my job today to set the stage for a more in-depth career discussion.* ➤ *I want to level-set my perceptions of my strengths and areas for improvement with my manager.* ➤ *I want to pitch my NeXtivity.* ➤ *Something else?* *What does success look like? Here are some examples:* ➤ *I want to learn about whether my boss and I see eye to eye about my performance.* ➤ *I want to hear my manager's feedback or feedforward on how I can improve in my current role so I can prepare to expand opportunities in the future.* ➤ *I want to hear what my manager thinks about my proposed development activity or pitch.* ➤ *I want to get a green light for my NeXtivity.* ➤ *Something else?*	

Step 3	Schedule your pitch with your manager. Here's an example of how to make the request:	Show appreciation for your manager's time.
	Email header: Free to chat next week?	
	"I would really appreciate your time for having a career conversation. My goal is to hear your perspective on my strengths and areas for improvement, and to share some ideas I have for a development activity that could help our team be more productive. Would you have time next Thursday for lunch or a coffee break, in-person or over the phone?"	State your goal. Show the win-win. Offer times to meet.
Step 4	Prepare the night before.	Get grounded in your VISION. Review your Best- Self cards. How do you want to show up? Review Week 4, WILL. Do a power pose, take a walk, get a great night's sleep.

DURING THE CAREER CONVERSATION WITH YOUR MANAGER

Step 5	Take the lead.	Bring a notebook. Prepare your pitch, questions and ideas of time.
	› Say *"Thanks for your time."*	
	› *State your goal or desired outcome. Ask your boss if he/she agrees or if there is something else to add.*	
	› *Fulfill your goal. Here are examples of things you could say or do:*	Watch for your "dinosaur brain" triggers.
	» *Calibrate how you are in your current role. Ask for feedforward.*	
	» *Tell your boss what you've learned through the weeks of exploring your VIEW.*	
	» *Pitch your NeXtivity if you think the timing is right. Ask "What do you think about this? What might make this work?"*	
	› *Take notes.*	
	› *Summarize your insights and agreements from the conversation.*	
	› *State action steps and timing.*	
	› *Before the meeting ends, schedule a time in both of your calendars for a follow-up conversation.*	

AFTER THE CAREER CONVERSATION WITH YOUR MANAGER

Step 6	Follow up on agreed-upon actions. Reflect on the conversation. Repeat STEP 1.	Revisit Week 4: WILL if you find yourself getting stuck or struggling to overcome your mountain.
	What went well? Not so well? What would you do differently next time?	

Be patient. You've got this. The blueprint is in your hands. You have everything you need to take charge of your VIEW.

FIRST, RECRUIT YOUR BOSS EXPERIENCE #15: COMMIT OR GO
Time: 25–35 mins.

How often do you think about leaving your current situation? Over 10,000 job switchers in a LinkedIn study said that "career opportunity" topped the list of reasons why they changed employers. Compensation, benefits and rewards came in last.[55] People jumped ship for different reasons, but many left when they stopped learning.

Perhaps you are convinced that your current work situation is an asset and that you owe it to yourself to make the most of the development opportunities it offers before you leave for greener pastures. But maybe you're really struggling to figure it out.

CONSIDER THESE REASONS TO STAY OR GO:
You might COMMIT if:

- You had a great pitch/career conversation with your boss and you're on your way to implementing or expanding your NeXtivity.

- Your boss is open to your ideas and NeXtivity. You feel there's a good chance to make things happen and you're willing to keep learning and trying.

- The organization is awesome. You think you may be able to explore opportunities with other managers or groups.

- You still feel like you are learning and growing; you have a chance to use your strengths every day.

- You're building great relationships with people in other departments or groups who can mentor and offer advice.

- Financially, it will cause more stress or unmanageable financial burden to leave.

- You have a chance to attend trainings or certifications that build your skills and credibility for the NeXtivity you'd like to create.

TIP > MIND-SET

Don't think of yourself as leaving your current situation.

Think of yourself as moving toward your VIEW.

You might GO if:

- You've made at least three substantial attempts to work with your manager to chart a NeXtivity and feel like you are getting nowhere or are going backward.

- You're experiencing physical or emotional stress as a result of the job or situation.

- You've lost the passion for your work or organization; your skills aren't being fully utilized and you've made many efforts over the past months but don't seem to be making progress.

- Your attitude and energy about your current situation are so low, you can't pick them back up. You may be hurting yourself more by staying.

- Sometimes, people in entry-level jobs in an organization, such as administrators, have a hard time breaking through people's perceptions of them as support staff. If this is the case for you, it's sometimes helpful to seek a fresh start in a different organization where you can re-create yourself.

- On the other hand, sometimes a person has been with an organization for so long he or she has a difficult time changing people's perceptions or trying new skills. Sometimes, a new beginning helps you re-create yourself.

If you decide to leave or make a big change in your current situation, here are some tips for making it a great experience:

- Embrace a positive mindset: Don't think of yourself as leaving a job, workplace or other situation. Think of yourself as moving toward something more aligned with your VIEW.

- If you work inside an organization, before you make any final decisions to leave:

  » *Take advantage of resources it may offer to help alleviate the stress or improve the situation. For example, is there an Employee Assistance Program (EAP), helpful Human Resources partner or ombudsperson (professional mediator) who can offer insight, coaching or tools for improving the situation?*

  » *Look through internal job postings. Talk with an internal recruiter. Is there a job, department or manager that might be a better fit for your VIEW?*

  » *Can someone in your Mentoring Network help improve your situation?*

- Before you start searching for what's next, reflect on your experience with this situation.

  » *What did you like?*

  » *What would you want from your next work situation? What kind of organization do you want to work for or create?*

- Reflect on what you've learned. What do you feel grateful for? What lessons and new skills are you taking with you?

- Reflect on relationships that were mutually supportive and successful. And those that were not so successful. What will you keep doing when it comes to building relationships with colleagues in the next situation? What will you do differently?

- Tap in to your Mentoring Network to explore new opportunities. Even with all the great technology at your fingertips, you're more likely to find your NeXtivity through someone you know than through any other source. The most successful seekers find their next move through networking.

- If you are looking for a job in an organization, check out resources for job hunters, such as the networking and job-hunting websites.

- Once you've landed in a new place and are leaving your current situation, remember to:

  » *Thank people you've worked with.*

  » *Stay in touch through professional networking social media.*

TIP > IF YOU ARE SELF-EMPLOYED

You may think about this Experience from two perspectives:

> Your current clients. Not all clients or customers are equal. Some client relationships are rewarding beyond financial compensation. You enjoy the collaboration, feel respected and learn something valuable from the gig or project that supports your ongoing relevance and value in the marketplace. Other clients drain your time, energy and resources, in spite of the financial rewards. Consider the clients you want to commit to and with whom you want to strengthen relationships, and consider which ones you may want to say goodbye to.

> Your business. How are you feeling about being self-employed? Are you living your VIEW or moving away from the dreams that inspired you to strike out on your own in the first place? Consider your satisfaction with your business and self-employment: Is it time to redouble your commitment or to pursue other options?

FIRST, RECRUIT YOUR BOSS: WRAP-UP AND REFLECTION

You now have tools for recruiting your boss and other allies, as well as tips for choosing whether to commit or leave your current situation. This week, you:

- Prepared your NeXtivity pitch.

- Made your pitch.

- Decided to commit or go.

Practice Box >

> **Commit to One Daily "First, Recruit Your Boss" Practice**

A practice is something you do every day with the intention to improve.[56] Each day for the next seven days of work, do something that builds a more positive relationship with your boss. For example, notice something your boss has done well, write a note of positive feedback and cc your boss's manager; go out for coffee or lunch if you're working nearby; take a compassionate view of a decision you disagree with to be more understanding; share an interesting article.

Next Week: Your VIEW for Life

You're ready now for the final week of this journey: Owning your VIEW for life.

Your View for Life

Your most essential asset

is not your job

or even your VIEW.

It is YOU.

Your VIEW for Life

"THE COGNITION YOU'VE GOT UP THERE IN YOUR HEAD—your education and training—it's worth something," said Nobel Prize–winning economist Gary Becker. Your experience counts, he explained. It enriches your portfolio of qualities and skills, and helps you be more creative, productive and employable. He pointed out that 75-80 percent of your economic output, where you exchange your energy, talent and time for money, comes from your own human capital.[57]

You are in charge of your life and the career of your dreams. When you self-direct your career, you own and create work opportunities that are personally meaningful to you and great for your organization as well. You win, your organization wins and the world is a much better place because of it.

Does your work prepare you for the future? Your VIEW is both the key to fulfillment *and* the new job security. It is a personal, must-have resource for responding with intention and confidence to the velocity of change in the world.

With your VIEW, you can choose to be proactive, positive and prepared, instead of reactive and timid.

What happens next?

You are the chief architect of your VIEW. The blueprint is now in your hands. But that doesn't mean that it's set in stone. As you grow and change, so can your VIEW and your plans. In the Introduction, I invited you to work at your own pace. Here are some suggestions for making your VIEW a lifelong habit.

EXPERIENCE #16: YOUR REFLECTIONS

- Go back to a week of your choosing: VISION; INSIGHT; ENGAGEMENT; WILL; First, Recruit Your Boss. What's something you would change?

EXPERIENCE #17: YOUR DEEPER DIVE

- What's something you'd want to dig deeper into? Felt overwhelmed by? There's time; go back.

EXPERIENCE #18: YOUR LIFELONG PRACTICES

- It takes 30 days to learn a new habit. Of all the practices you've adopted, which one(s) did you stick with? Which one(s) resonated? Make a final commitment. Choose one practice from the previous five weeks or look through the curated list in the Appendix. Commit to this practice for the next six months, to embody your VIEW.

Before We Say Goodbye

"Contact" is my favorite movie of all time. Based on the best-selling book Cosmos, by Carl Sagan, it's the story of a brilliant woman astrophysicist named Eleanor Arroway, played by Jodie Foster, who believes she will find extraterrestrial intelligence. When she overcomes obstacles and the odds and makes her discovery, the very people who put roadblocks in her way try to take over her project. When she fulfills her dreams and meets the aliens, they appear to her in the form of her long-dead father. Most people choke up at the sight of the poignant father-daughter reunion. My eyes stay dry.

The scene that brings me to tears, each of the hundred or so times I've seen it, is the finale. Eleanor been called to testify before Congress about the journey she took to meet the extraterrestrials. But the video camera she brought on her mission couldn't handle the cosmic complexities of traveling through the time-and-space-collapsing wormhole that brought her from Earth to the aliens' part of the universe and back again in just 18 seconds. She returned with no pictures, no space rock or soil sample to prove she'd taken the trip. As a scientist, she was trained to believe in only the things for which there is irrefutable evidence. A panel of congressional investigators grills her for testimony; people around the world huddle around their TVs to watch. She realizes that even she would be skeptical of her story and struggles to prove she had this extraordinary experience.

We witness her internal battle between the scientific conviction that rules her reasoning and her inexpressible feelings about her journey. It's a battle of mind versus heart; science versus faith. She chooses her words slowly. Her eyes glisten with inspiration.

> *"I was given something wonderful, something that changed me forever. . . . A vision . . . of the universe that tells us, undeniably, how tiny and insignificant and how rare and precious we all are. A vision that tells us that we belong to something that is greater than ourselves, that we are not . . . that none of us are alone. I wish I could share that. . . . I wish that everyone, if only for one moment, could feel that awe and humility and hope. But . . . that continues to be my wish."*

I'm not saying we're heading for an alien planet, although through the vision and grit of business leaders and talented astroengineers, we will get to Mars sooner than we imagined. I am saying that we are in a new time in human history, a time of the greatest change and expansion that the world has ever seen.

We can choose to meet these new frontiers with awe, humility and hope. If leaders from all parts of life—business, government, healthcare, education, agriculture—choose a positive path, perhaps we can witness the greatest time in human history, when we actually solve the world's wickedest problems: hunger, violence, crippling health issues and disease. But we don't have to just rely on those leaders. We have ourselves and our VIEW. Change brings opportunity when you have the vision, passion and confidence to seize it and create, experiment and make.

"Nothing is a mistake. There's no win and no fail. There's only make." [58] —Sister Corita Kent

Maybe like Eleanor Arroway, it will be hard for you to talk with others about your experience, to articulate your vision, your VIEW. Some people won't understand. Others will discourage you from taking risks. You have the WILL to choose whom you will accept encouragement and coaching from, and whom you will offer a polite "thank you." Your job title doesn't matter. You can choose to lead yourself. When you choose with confidence and intention, others will follow.

You have been given something wonderful: the unique gifts and qualities that make you who you are. They did not exist before you were born and will not come again when you leave. Remember to ask yourself, What brings meaning and purpose to your life? How does work fit in?

Your most important asset in this journey is YOU.

It is my wish that you use your VIEW for your own fulfillment and as a ballast for any turbulence that finds its way into your life or work. Reach for to your VIEW. By being your best, authentic self, you will make this world a better place.

RESOURCES

INSIGHT EXPERIENCE: YOUR BEST SELF
Low-tech version

If you are unable to download the card set for the Best Self Experience, you can work from this list instead. (Please note that this is a different list from the Signature Skills Experience, which has a different focus and purpose.)

> To prepare for this Experience, you will need:
> - *A timer.*
> - *A pencil or pen.*
> - *A spare sheet of paper.*

1. **Your gut is your guidance system.** The sort should be a flow, where you instinctively react to each word. Work quickly. This is the reason for the five-minute timer, to help you avoid overthinking.

2. **Read the following directions before you begin,** so you know where you are heading.

3. **Set a timer to five minutes.** Do not go over the five minutes! I have led this exercise with hundreds of people and, while most people say they feel overwhelmed at the beginning, they also say that it gets easier and more time wouldn't have changed their result.

4. **Review the list of qualities and traits.** Cross out the ones that do not resonate for you.

5. **Go back over the list** and put a check mark next to the qualities that resonate.

6. **Pare the list** down to 16 qualities.

7. **Using a piece of scrap paper, write the 16 qualities in a diamond formation,** with the most important trait at the top; the next two, three, four; then three, two and the quality "least" important of your top 16, as in the example on the previous page.

Accurate	Amiable	Authentic
Aware	Careful	Caring
Change Catalyst	Charismatic	Coach
Collaborative	Collegial	Communicative
Compassionate	Competent	Composed
Confident	Consistent	Creative
Critical Thinker	Curious	Customer-focused

Decisive	Delegator	Diligent
Disciplined	Effective	Emotionally Intelligent
Empathetic	Encouraging	Ethical
Flexible	Fun	Hands-on
Honest	Imaginative	Inclusive
Influential	Innovative	Insightful
Just	Kind	Knowledgeable
Likeable	Listener	Logical
Mentor	Mindful	Motivator
Open to Change	Open-Minded	Optimistic
Organized	Persuasive	Practical
Pragmatic	Proactive	Problem-Solver
Productive	Resilient	Resonant
Resourceful	Respectful	Results-Oriented
Savvy	Self-Aware	Selfless
Strategic	Superstar	Supportive
Systematic	Systems Thinker	Team Player
Thorough	Thoughtful	Trail-Blazer
Trustworthy	Unique	Useful
Versatile	Visionary	Wise

Ideas for goal setting:

If you want to...	Then write a...	Examples to get you started
Find more flow or increase your happiness	Work Enjoyment Goals	➤ *Do more work activities that give me enjoyment, and a sense of satisfaction or flow* ➤ *Focus more on the things that I can control or influence* ➤ *Improve my health* ➤ *Develop more supportive relationships with work colleagues.* ➤ *My idea:*

Change how you act	Behavioral Goals	▸ *Develop a skill for greater emotional intelligence, such as,*
		» *Be more empathetic*
		» *Become a better listener*
		» *Handle conflict more effectively*
		» *Gain self-awareness of my hot buttons and learn to manage them*
		» *Develop more resilience*
		» *Demonstrate composure in challenging situations*
		▸ *Live a healthier lifestyle:*
		» *Exercise more*
		» *Eat healthier*
		» *Manage stress more effectively*
		▸ *Take breaks or vacations more frequently to refresh and renew*
		▸ *Spend more time with family or friends*
		▸ *Be more effective at influencing and motivating others, whether they report to me or not*
		▸ *Make a point each day to interact with more of the people I manage and lead*
		▸ *Learn to influence more effectively*
		▸ *Seek input more regularly on a project or task*
		▸ *Foster my creativity*
		▸ *My idea:*

Move into another role, department or organization or if you are wondering if it's time for you to hang up your own shingle or start a new business	Movement Goals	▸ *Earn a promotion* ▸ *Move into senior leadership* ▸ *Become a manager* ▸ *Become a board member* ▸ *Start my own business* ▸ *My idea:*
Broaden your exposure to other people, places or experiences	Expansion Goals	▸ *Incorporate more responsibilities for people and/or tasks into my current role* ▸ *Build more relationships and network more inside and/or outside of the organization* ▸ *Get visibility internally and/or externally* ▸ *Meet more decision makers* ▸ *Learn about what someone does in another department* ▸ *Find a mentor* ▸ *Mentor someone else* ▸ *Create a professional website or blog* ▸ *Build my "personal brand"* ▸ *My idea:*

Learn a new skill or pick up new information	Skill Goals	<ul><li>*Think more strategically*</li><li>*Delegate more effectively*</li><li>*Improve decision-making capability*</li><li>*Develop negotiation skills*</li><li>*Become a more compelling public speaker or presenter*</li><li>*Improve a technical skill*</li><li>*Present more effectively*</li><li>*Communicate more effectively*</li><li>*Learn a new language*</li><li>*Learn a new market or geography*</li><li>*My idea:*</li></ul>
Improve your performance; do something more effectively, efficiently, productively	Performance Goals	<ul><li>*Prioritize competing projects more effectively*</li><li>*Reallocate 2–20 percent of the time and energy spent in my current role to more productive tasks*</li><li>*Improve by a specific, measurable percent (e.g., double productivity; improve sales outcomes by 10 percent)*</li><li>*My idea:*</li></ul>

ACKNOWLEDGMENTS

For helping to bring this book into the world, my heartfelt thanks to Sue Barlow, Angela Nannini, Emily Weece, Stacey Cassat-Green, Sari Boren, Deborah Sosin, and Amy Humble. With gratitude for my teachers at GrubStreet, Boston, especially Ethan Gilsdorf, Alexandria Marzano-Lesnevich, Pagan Kennedy, Michelle Seaton and Jennifer Crystal. For all my Grubbies, especially Beth Altringer, Debbie Blicher, Sari Boren, Claire Cheney, Molly Howes, Kevin O'Kelly, Katie Pakos Rimer, Rebecca Rollins, Kat Setzer, Carroll Sandel, Shelby Meyerhoff, Christine Cooper, Meg Newhouse and Caroline Keene. For the visionary Eve Bridburg, GrubStreet's founder. I am amazed by your talents and have learned from you all.

For reviewing the manuscript with fresh eyes: Tim Hall, Eileen Pyne, Bob Melendy, Alan Frohman, Kathy Baron, Donna Prior-Fonseca and Nancy Persson. You made the book stronger. For Jack McCarthy and EDRT colleagues, who share my belief that good leaders in organizations can create a better world. You are my partners in learning. And for Lucy Tshuka and Emily Friedman, who pushed me to think more critically and whose passion for this work matches my own. The journey would not have been the same without you.

For advice, friendship and support, heartfelt thanks to: David Baron, Tim Huggins, Sara DiVello, Gary Cohen, Perry Carrison, Glen Morris, Michelle Toth, Miriam Adams, Mary Cotton and Jamie Clarke; Diane, Jonathan and Sula Fassino-Miller. To Cigdem Oktem, Ellen Di Resta and Kathleen Federico for hosting the first readings. For support in the early stages of writing this book, deep appreciation for Stephanie Clayman, Gail Deegan, Gail Snowden, Annie Braudy, Jennifer Mattson and Maggie Keller. For listening, feedback and friendship, gratitude to my Neighborhood Book Group and my Pinktank pals. The word restaurant means "food that restores" in French. Heartfelt thanks to Afkham and the team at L'Aroma Cafe for their great coffee and welcoming retreat when I ran out steam. Also, to Lana, Olya and Lilly at The Rox; and to Eunice and Steve Feller. Good food and company are good for the soul.

For their inspiration and contributions to the field of leadership and career development: Tim Hall, Marcia Hyatt, Betsy Collard, and Cliff Hakim. For Carolyn Carder, Susie Rheault, Ruth Parham, Chris Coffin, Sandra Drought, and Susan Ennis for their mentorship early in my career, which has opened so much opportunity since. For my guardian angels, the Santos family, especially Ana; as well as Betsey Stone, Helena de Silva, and Fadime Schlosser. To George Nadaff, who rented an office to me where I found the space I needed to write. And for Kurt Lewin, founding father of social psychology, who believed in a more compassionate world. His spirit inspires me every day literally and in practice as I wrote portions of this book in his former home, where my family now lives.

For my cheerleaders and sister-friends, for reading, feedback, ideas and strong shoulders: Paula Hall, Diane Baron, Mary Katherine Fallon, Marguerite Fletcher, Carolyn Eggert, Brooke Baker and Marianne Ganley. And for Sandy Connors, Helen Ventouris, Susan Poole, Susan Veroff, Martha Wells, Liz Massicotte and Monica Kinney-Houde, who keep me smiling. I love you all. With love to my family for lifelong support: Veronica and Paul Rochefort, Kathy and Jack Prior, Ginger Rierdan, Joanna and Joseph Holt, the Cheshire Priors, the Ohio Bernards, Vicki Hopewell and Rebecca Batchie, and all the cousins.

For my parents, Ginny and Joe Bucciaglia, and brothers, Paul and Joe, for their unconditional love, kindness and support. You are my touchstones.

For my treasures, Jack, Kayla and Jared Prior, who fill me with pride and tolerate frozen pizza for dinner. And for Allie, Lucy, Kay and Artemis, for wags, purrs and walks.

ENDNOTES

1. Bruce Springsteen, *Born to Run* (New York: Simon & Schuster, 2016), p. 401.

2. Department of Labor, Bureau of Labor Statistics, "American Time Use Survey Summary," June 2016. http://www.bls.gov/news.release/atus.nr0.htm, downloaded December 12, 2016.

3. Richard Dobbs, James Manyika, Jonathan Woetzel McKinsey, "The Four Global Forces Breaking All the Trends," McKinsey Global Institute, April 2015. http://www. mckinsey.com/business-functions/strategy-and-corporate-finance/our-insights/the-four-global-forces-breaking-all-the-trends, downloaded December 12, 2016.

4. Cliff Hakim, *We Are All Self-Employed: The New Social Contract for Working in a Changed World* (San Francisco: Berrett-Koehler, 1994).

5. Mary O'Hara-Devereaux, "Demographics Are Destiny—Healthy Longevity and Women's Second Middle Age," YouTube video. https://www.bing.com/videos/search?q=mary+o%27hara-devereaux&view=detail&mid=83ED0293699A38881B9D83ED0293699A38881B9D&FORM=VIRE, downloaded July 14, 2016.

6. James Flaherty, *Coaching: Evoking Excellence in Others*, Third Edition (New York: Routledge, 2014), p. 178. Printed with permission.

7. Adapted from Cynthia D. McCauley et al., *Experience-Driven Leader Development: Models, Tools, Best Practices, and Advice for On-the-Job Development*, First Edition (San Francisco: Wiley, 2014), pp. 250–251.

8. Personal Interview with Erin Judge, January 2009. Printed with permission.

9. Carolyn Gregoire, "Why Your Best Ideas Happen in the Most Unusual Places," *Huffington Post*, September 8, 2013; and Shelley Carson, "When Being Distracted Is a Good Thing," *Huffington Post*, March 4, 2012. http://www.huffingtonpost.com/2013/09/08/best-ideas-unusual-places_n_3824660.html; http://www.shelleycarson.com/blog/when-being-distracted-is-a-good-thing.

10. Jon Briscoe, Douglas T. Hall, Wolfgang Mayrhofer, *Careers Around the World: Individual and Contextual Perspectives* (New York: Routledge, 2011), p. 76.

11. Ibid.

12. Joe Dominguez and Vicki Robin, *Your Money or Your Life: Transforming Your Relationship with Money and Achieving Financial Independence* (New York: Penguin Books, 1999), p. 55. Reprinted with permission.

13. Daniel Pink, *A Whole New Mind: Why Right-Brainers Will Rule the Future* (New York: Riverhead Books, 2006, Rep Upd edition), p. 54. Reprinted with permission.

14. Philip Kennicott, "Daniel Pink and the Economic Model of Creativity," *Washington Post*, April 2, 2008. http://www.washingtonpost.com/wp-dyn/content/article/2008/04/01/AR2008040102435.html, downloaded July 17, 2016.

15. Flaherty, p. 178

16. Laura M. Roberts et al., "Composing the Reflected Best Self Portrait: Building Pathways for Becoming Extraordinary in Work Organizations," *Academy of Management Review* 2005, Vol. 30, No. 4, pp. 712–736.

17. Briscoe et al., pp. 65–66.

18. Daniel M. Cable et al., "How Best-Self Activation Influences Emotions, Physiology and Employment Relationships." *Harvard Business School Working Paper*, No. 16-029, September 2015.

19. Amy Cuddy, *Presence: Bringing Your Boldest Self to Your Biggest Challenges* (New York: Little, Brown and Company, 2015), p. 50.

20. VIA Institute on Character, "Signature Strengths" (summary of research findings, retrieved at http://www.viacharacter.org/www/Research/What-the-Research-Says-About-Character-Strengths-Signature-Strengths); and Hadassah Littman-Ovadia, Vered Lazar-Butbul, Benny Benjamin, "Strengths-Based Career Counseling: Overview and Initial Evaluation, *Journal of Career Assessment* 2014, Vol. 22, No. 3, pp. 403–419; and René T. Proyer et al., "Strengths-Based Positive Psychology Interventions: A Randomized Placebo-Controlled Online Trial on Long-Term Effects for a Signature Strengths- vs. a Lesser-Strengths Intervention," *Frontiers in Psychology,* 2015, 6:456. http://www.viacharacter.org/www/Research/What-the-Research-Says-About-Character-Strengths-Signature-Strengths; and

21. From "Stop Overdoing Your Strengths," by Robert E. Kaplan; Robert B. Kaiser. *Harvard Business Review*, February 2009. Reprinted with permission.

22. Jim Taylor and Gregory Scott Wilson, *Applying Sport Psychology: Four Perspectives* (Champaign, IL: Human Kinetics, 2005).

23. Carol Dweck, *Mindset: The New Psychology of Success* (New York: Ballantine, 2007), p. 11. Reprinted with permission.

24. Albert J. Bernstein, *Dinosaur Brains: Dealing with All THOSE Impossible People at Work* (New York: Ballantine, 1996).

25. Adapted from Douglas Stone and Sheila Heen, *Thanks for the Feedback: The Science and Art of Receiving Feedback Well* (New York: Penguin Books, 2015).

26. Excerpt from QUIET: THE POWER OF INTROVERTS IN A WORLD THAT CAN'T STOP TALKING by Susan Cain, copyright © 2012, 2013 by Susan Cain. Used by permission of Crown Books, an imprint of the Crown Publishing Group, a division of Penguin Random House LLC. All rights reserved. Any third party use of this material, outside of this publication, is prohibited. Interested parties must apply directly to Penguin Random House LLC for permission," p. 143.

27. Flaherty, p. 178.

28. VIA Institute on Character, "Signature Strengths." http://www.viacharacter.org/www/Research/What-the-Research-Says-About-Character-Strengths-Signature-Strengths.

29. Mihaly Csikszentmihalyi, *The Psychology of Optimal Experience* (New York: Harper Classics, 2008), p. 6.

30. Mihaly Csikszentmihalyi, TED2004; https://www.ted.com/talks/mihaly_ csikszentmihalyi_on_flow, downloaded January 2, 2017. Printed with permission.

31. Ibid.

32. Lisa Prior, "Organizational Career Development Savvy," Boston University Executive Development Roundtable, Boston University Questrom Graduate School of Management, 1997.

33. American Psychological Association Help Center, "What You Need to Know about Willpower: The Psychological Science of Self-Control," http://www.apa.org/helpcenter/willpower.aspx, downloaded September 4, 2016.

34. Ibid.

35. American Psychological Association Help Center, "Is Willpower a Limited Resource?" https://www.apa.org/helpcenter/willpower-limited-resource.pdf, downloaded September 4, 2016.

36. Jeremy Adam Smith, "Three Benefits to Mindfulness at Work," *The Greater Good: Science of a Meaningful Life* Newsletter, November 17, 2014. http://greatergood.berkeley.edu/article/item/three_benefits_to_mindfulness_at_work.

37. Karen Reivich and Andrew Shatte, *The Resilience Factor: 7 Keys to Finding Your Inner Strength and Overcoming Life's Hurdles* (New York: Broadway Books, 2003), p. 290.

38. Carol Dweck, "What Having a 'Growth Mindset' Actually Means," *Harvard Business Review,* January 2016. https://hbr.org/2016/01/what-having-a-growth-mindset-actually-means, downloaded September 8, 2016.

39. Art Markman, "What Makes Us Thankful," *The Greater Good: Science of a Meaningful Life Newsletter,* April 20, 2015, http://greatergood.berkeley.edu/article/item/what_makes_us_thankful, downloaded September 3, 2016.

40. Shawn Anchor, *The Happiness Advantage: The Seven Principles of Positive Psychology that Fuel Success and Performance at Work* (New York: Crown Business, 2010), p. 21. Reprinted with permission.

41. Wendy Palmer, *Search Outside Yourself,* "Leadership Embodiment" blog post; http://www.embodimentinternational.com/search-outside-yourself-by-wendy-palmer/ downloaded September 7, 2016.

42. Kathy E. Kram and Monica C. Higgins, "A New Mindset on Mentoring: Creating Developmental Networks at Work," *MIT Sloan Management Review,* April 15, 2009.

43. Briscoe et al., p. 173.

44. "What Is Mindfulness?" *The Greater Good: Science of a Meaningful Life Newsletter,* undated. http://greatergood.berkeley.edu/topic/mindfulness/definition

45. Executive Development Round Table (EDRT) Spring Conference 2016, a partnership between the Questrom School of Management at Boston University and the Center for Creative Leadership. The author was a steering committee member at the time of this writing. Printed with permission.

46. EDRT conference, Fall 2015 and website https://www.nd.edu/features/your-brain-on-sleep/ downloaded September 6, 2016. Printed with permission.

47. Robert Half, "Insomnia and Performance of US Workers," 2016 reported by Robert Half, Accountemps, 2016.

48. Wendy Palmer and Janet Crawford, "Leadership Embodiment: How the Way We Sit and Stand Can Change the Way We Think and Speak," CreateSpace, an Amazon Company, October 12, 2013, p. 4.

49. Cuddy, p. 53.

50. Amy Cuddy, "Your Body Language Shapes Who You Are," TED Talk, https://www.ted.com/talks/amy_cuddy_your_body_language_shapes_who_you_are?language=en downloaded September 4, 2016.

51. Cuddy, p. 228.

52. Flaherty, p. 178.

53. Barbara Kiviat, "Jobs Are the New Assets," *Time,* March 12, 2009. http://content.time.com/time/specials/packages/article/0,28804,1884779_1884782_1884749,00.html.

54. Briscoe et al., p. 76; and personal interview with author Douglas T. Hall, Morton H. and Charlotte Friedman Professor in Management, Organizational Behavior Department, Boston University Questrom School of Business, November 7, 2016.

55. Allison Schnidman, "New Research Reveals the Real Reason People Switch Jobs, and It Isn't Money or Their Boss," LinkedIn Talent Blog, August 5, 2015. https://business.linkedin.com/talent-solutions/blog/2015/08/new-research-reveals-the-real-reason-people-switch-jobs-and-it-isnt-money-or-their-boss , downloaded March 14, 2016.

56. Flaherty, p. 178.

57. Kiviat, March 12, 2009. http://content.time.com/time/specials/packages/article/0,28804,1884779_1884782_1884749,00.html.

58. From Sister Corita Kent, from *10 Rules for Students, Teachers and Life*, downloaded from https://www.brainpickings.org/2012/08/10/10-rules-for-students-and-teachers-john-cage-corita-kent/. ??

If you'd like to continue receiving practical tips about leadership, change and career development, please visit my website at **www.priorconsulting.com** and sign up for my newsletter. You can also connect with me on LinkedIn, Twitter and through the T*ake Charge of Your VIEW* Facebook page. If this journey was helpful, please let us know on Amazon.com!

43789173R10104

Made in the USA
Middletown, DE
19 May 2017